Praise for BE KNOWN FOR SOMETHING

"The Church is the body of Christ on Earth to meet the needs of a broken world. But how do churches communicate and connect to a world that is blinded by sin and resistant to the gospel? God has gifted Mark MacDonald with an ability to bring the two together. Any church that is intentional about reaching people outside their walls needs the insights offered in this book."

Dr. Mel Blackaby
Senior Pastor, First Baptist Church (Jonesboro, GA)

"This is the book the church needs. Mark gives church leaders a roadmap to church health and community engagement. Take the time to read and absorb this book. Your church and community depend on it!"

Andy Swart
Lead and Founding Pastor, Metro Church (NW Arkansas)

"Every few years, I come across a great team read for my staff or board — then, I can't find another for a long while. Well, this is the motherlode, jackpot, unbeatable win for a staff and board team-read. It's going to make future picks even more difficult! Thanks to the practical insights and the discussion starters at the end of each chapter, we're discovering exactly how to be known for something that really matters!"

Kevin J. Matthews
Lead Pastor, The Point Church (New Brunswick, Canada)

"Mark specializes in people, and he knows how to help people find their one thing. Do you want to be known for something? Read *Be Known for Something*."

Dr. Rob Peters

Senior Pastor, Calvary Baptist Church & Day School
(Winston-Salem, NC)

"This book gives church leaders the insights needed to unearth, clarify, and communicate to the world why your organization matters and can make a difference in their lives. Stop wasting energy on tactics that over-promise and under-deliver, and get to the heart of how to pinpoint your message. Mark makes the path clear."

Tommy Brown

Minister, Author, Speaker
The Seven Money Types

"Many of us (myself included) become church communicators without formal training. We pick up a few things along the way, but when we try to learn more, we're often met with complicated lingo and examples that don't seem relevant to the work we do. Mark MacDonald has solved this problem in his new book, *Be Known for Something*. With clear language and engaging storytelling, he walks through marketing principles that will help you identify what makes your church unique and leverage those qualities to reach and engage people in your community."

Lori Bailey

Central Group Leader of Communications
Life.Church

"Mark's experience with helping churches rediscover what they are known for shines through in his book. These principles will guide your church team as you seek to know your community and your neighbors; and as you remember why God called the church into existence. It's not about us!"

Andrew Myers

Communications Manager,
Canadian Baptists of Atlantic Canada

"Mark provides outstanding leadership as churches search for their identity among their attendees and their surrounding communities. His team's insights, creativity, and assistance in the process are invaluable. This book finally puts that process in writing!"

Dr. Joe Carbonaro

Executive Director, Kingwood United Methodist Church
(Kingwood, TX)

"Mark MacDonald is known for being an extraordinary communicator with a heart for the ministry of the church. He is exceptionally gifted at helping ministry leaders work through the mission and vision God has placed on their heart to develop a strategic communication strategy. This book is a great tool for any ministry leader to make Jesus known in your community."

Micah Ferguson

Director of Strategic Initiatives,
Florida Baptist Convention

"This book is a game-changer for churches and leaders who are searching for how they can more effectively reach their community. Mark's book is practical, insightful, and will become the playbook for churches to be known for something."

Phil Bowdle
Creative Arts Pastor, West Ridge Church (Georgia)

"Mark's creative skill and communication prowess is uncommon; however, what makes the space he dwells in rarified air is that he puts the full force of who he is into the work of building the local church. Like a magnifying glass on a sidewalk ant, this level of focus will light your church on fire in the best sense of the word. For churches large and small, this is more than a must read. It is a must-implement set of best practices honed through Mark's years of experience working in and with local churches."

Dan Lidstone
Creative Director, Harvest Bible Chapel (Chicago, IL)

"Is your church known for something? Mark does such a great job in this book of helping simply and clearly to lay out a plan for your church to be known for the thing that makes you unique and special! I wish I would have had this book when I was getting started in church communications! If you have not figured out what you are known for and how to share that with you community, please read this right now!"

Stephen Brewster
Executive Creative Pastor, Freedom House Church (Charlotte, NC)

"*Be Known for Something* is an essential, go-to guide for finding your unique calling as a church. Have you ever wondered what you are known for in your community? Mark MacDonald poses compelling observations and offers insightful solutions for the church craving clarity and a path to improve their reputation in the community."

Gerry True

Minister of Communication Arts, Oak Hills Church (Texas)

"When it comes to helping churches figure out how to position themselves for maximum impact in their communities, nobody is a bigger expert than Mark MacDonald. And now, he's dumped his brain into this handy resource for us. If you want to determine what you want to be known for, this is a must-read! Do yourself a favor and grab a highlighter because this is going to be a workbook that you're going to want to come back to again and again!"

Chuck Scoggins

Executive Director, Center for Church Communication

"Mark brings contagious enthusiasm and deep insight to every conversation, speaking engagement, and teaching opportunity. *Be Known for Something* promises to do the same. His ability to reveal communication truths to marketers and non-marketers alike in fresh and engaging ways keeps audiences laughing while they learn to improve their organizations' reputation and message. I'm grateful for his friendship and constant encouragement."

Evan McBroom

Chief Culture Officer, Founder, & Partner
Fishhook

"Mark's teaching is inspired, and his heart for ministry is evident in his writing. This book is great for church communicators and pastors alike, whether they've been serving for years or a day."

Katie Allred

Co-Founder, Church Communications Facebook Group
Web Content Manager, Brentwood Baptist Church

"Mark MacDonald is a person of passion for church people and the mission of congregations. He has connected, changed, and energized people of faith to communicate clearly their unique message. Now, you can hold that energy in your hand with his book. *Be Known for Something* will guide you through a process that can energize your ministry connection to your community... every team and congregation should grab a copy and begin the journey."

Phill Martin

Deputy CEO, The Church Network

"Mark MacDonald has a unique ability to communicate and guide churches to think differently about what they are intentionally and unintentionally communicating to the outside world. *Be Known for Something* translates his knowledge onto paper in an informal but compelling fashion that will challenge and guide church leaders on how they can truly be 'known' for something."

Jim Wagner

Managing Director/Publisher,
Worship Facilities Conference and Expo,
Worship Facilities Magazine

"Mark MacDonald offers an insightful look at the current condition of the 21st century church, and he crafts a clear path forward for the church to alter its socially-constructed and programmatically-additive approach toward a more intentional purpose of being known for something. We often neglect the role that perception plays in how people view the church, its leadership, and its members, which leads to individuals outside the church acting as if that perception is reality. Mark's background and expertise in communication help church leaders to realign their priorities for the church."

Darren P. Lawson

Dean, School of Fine Arts and Communication
Bob Jones University

"When it comes to getting new people to visit your church, reputation is everything. How people perceive your church and talk about it is what determines whether more people will come. In a world where the church is known more for what we are against, Mark challenges us and gives us the practical steps to revitalize the church's reputation so we are known for something far more authentic. This book will help you find that unique thread you must embrace to connect again with your community and grow your church."

Justin Dean

Co-Founder, *That Church* Conference
Author, *PR Matters: A Survival Guide for Church Communicators*

"Mark MacDonald is spearheading must-needed change with *Be Known For Something*, helping churches navigate the biggest communication shift our world has seen in the last 500 years."

Brady Shearer
CEO, Pro Church Tools

"Mark truly is one of the most intuitive and creative people I know... his love for Jesus and passion for helping others effectively communicate the gospel to our lost world is brilliantly contagious."

Stu Epperson, Jr.
Author, *Last Words of Jesus & First Words of Jesus*
President, Truth Network

"Thankfully, Mark wastes no time talking about the marketing and branding that's hurting your church. Even better? He moves past the problem fast to get to the good stuff—what to do about it. I didn't even get through page 15 before grabbing my favorite pen to start taking notes and answering questions. Reading this book is like sitting down with one of your trusted best buds. You know the one... the friend who has a way of helping you see and fix what's broken in perceptions and reality. Mark's THAT guy. He makes the hard, complicated stuff easy and fun. Enjoy the process. You have everything to gain by sitting down with the help this ad man, actor, and model is making available to you and your church."

Kem Meyer
Author of and Advocate, *Less Chaos. Less Noise: Effective Communications for an Effective Church*

BE KNOWN
FOR
SOMETHING

RECONNECT WITH COMMUNITY BY
REVITALIZING YOUR CHURCH'S REPUTATION

MARK MACDONALD

HIGH BRIDGE BOOKS
HOUSTON

Be Known for Something
by Mark MacDonald

Printed in the United States of America
ISBN (Paperback): 978-1-940024-98-1
ISBN (eBook): 978-1-940024-99-8

High Bridge Books titles may be purchased in bulk for educational, business, fundraising, or sales promotional use. For information please contact High Bridge Books via www.HighBridgeBooks.com/contact.

Published in Houston, Texas by High Bridge Books

DEDICATION

To the pastor, ministry leader, church communication director, deacon, and media dude (or dudette) who is truly seeking to follow passionately after our Savior and make a difference in the world. This book is dedicated to taking your work to the next level of effectiveness. Empowered with the amazing gifts of eternal grace and mercy that only Jesus offers, may we be known for mirroring Him.

Thank you, Tammy, my forever partner who fanned the flames of my dreams and encouraged me to write this book. I love you.

I'm humbled by my sons, Joshua and Isaac, who remind me daily how important it is to get life's choices right. I watch as a proud father as you both work in ministry for our Heavenly Father.

I'm thankful also to my true-friend relationships and the countless life experiences that shape who I am.

Because of them and Him, I share these stories.

—*Mark*

CONTENTS

FOREWORD

A man once asked me, "Where do you go to church?"

I responded, "Calvary Baptist."

To which, he replied, "You mean that rich church on Country Club Road?"

A little surprised, I said, "Well, I don't know if we are rich, but yes, we are located on Country Club Road."

I had never thought of our church as "the rich church," but obviously, that was the perception of at least one man in our city. I wondered if there were others who had the same impression. I thought, "Perhaps we should change our address to Peacehaven Road, which was on the other side of our property." That sounded much more like what I thought our church is about, speaking the peace of God into the brokenness of our community.

I realized that my perception may not be the way others see our church. Most church members see their church in a positive light (unless they are in the midst of a church squabble). However, the real question is this: How do people in the community view our church? What are their impressions of who we are and what we do?

If you want to do a really brave act of courage, ask a friend who is not in your church if he/she would be willing to help you by doing an informal community survey. Give them a clip board with paper and ask them to approach people in their normal flow of life and say the following:

I've been asked to do a survey to discover how people in the community view the church on the corner. [Or, give the name of the church if the building is not in view.] I have three questions. Would you be willing to give me your opinion? Your answers will be totally anonymous.

Here are the three questions:

- Have you ever attended that church?
- Do you know anyone who attends that church?
- What are your impressions of that church?

If they complete 10 to 20 interviews, you will likely get a fairly good idea of how people outside your church perceive you. You may find that they have no idea what you do besides meet on Sundays. Or, they may say, "I think they care about the homeless. I understand they provide shelter for the homeless in the winter." Or, "I understand they have classes to help people with their marriages. A friend of mine once invited me, but I didn't go because we were not having any problems."

Many churches are not connecting with their community. They have become safe havens for church members but have little attraction for the non-church community.

The book you are about to read will help you evaluate who you are now, what you should be doing, and how to communicate it effectively in order to engage your community. More importantly, it will help you "be known for something." Mark MacDonald will take you through the re-discovery steps and show you how to reconnect to the community where God has placed you.

If you are a pastor or other church leader, you may want to use this as a study tool for your team, committee, or board. If you are ready to grow, this book will point the way.

Gary Chapman, Ph.D.
Author, *The 5 Love Languages*

INTRODUCTION

I was introduced to an important client many years ago. I was just starting my advertising and marketing communication career. They seemed like a normal organization, so when I heard what they were doing, I was perplexed. Talking to their managers and leaders, they were truly interested in the people who followed them, and they worked long, hard hours to provide a product that people needed. And those same people seemed to love them back. Their product seemed to be needed (especially when you read the newspapers and watch the trends of their surrounding communities).

The mystery deepened.

With all this good going on, they had a problem. In fact, it was a potentially terminal problem. And if they ignored it much longer, it would lead to their failure and demise.

This client? The Church.

Don't get me wrong. I actually was introduced to the Church (the big "C," global group of Christ-followers) in my preschool years when my parents attended a small fellowship near my childhood home with my sister, brother, and me. Just before I started kindergarten, our family moved to another community, and we started to attend another local church.

I don't really remember that move, but we started going to a church that had recently hired a new, dynamic pastor who would transform a small, suburban church into a large and growing ministry that allowed our entire family to minister and grow spiritually. It was there at the age of eight that I truly joined the

Church when I realized my life needed a Savior to give it worth, direction, forgiveness, and a destination.

A couple of decades later, I would reintroduce myself to this client.

I thought every church was like my home church. But they're not. I did what I did with any new account; I sought to learn everything I could possibly discover about it. The more I looked, the more I saw issues.

The Church was and is losing influence in the community. The Church, the entire wonderful collection of believers in Jesus Christ, is drifting into obscurity. Remember the last commandment of Christ? He told us that, as we're going about life, we're to share the amazing life that can be found in becoming a disciple of Him. Over the last several decades, the Church has been shrinking in size... and impact. We haven't been practicing the Great Commission effectively.

The Church isn't known for something.

Since the mid-'80s, I've worked with large and small advertising, branding, and marketing agencies. The more I've lived in the agency world, the more I've realized what's missing. It's the blind spot of most churches. They lack a clearly stated benefit.

Don't get me wrong. The people who are in the Church know the benefit of following Jesus... the fellowship, sanctification, joy, peace... and the list goes on and on. We meet regularly to bask in the benefits. But the world has no clue what we have. And the trend seems to be clear now: the world's increasing in size, but the Church isn't. Our communities are growing while the local churches are plateauing or shrinking. Perhaps the average believer doesn't truly know the benefits as clearly as we'd think. We promote the latest mobile app that we've recently discovered faster than the benefits of joining the family of God.

But it's not just the Church. We all want more influence. In order to accomplish the Great Commission successfully through our day-to-day tasks, we *need* to have more influence.

We all need to be known for something.

In my life, I've been known for being a...

singer,
son,
actor,
liar,
artist,
model,
salesperson,
student,
designer,
production manager,
husband,
father,
art director,
author,
business owner,
friend,
branding guy,
speaker,
sinner,
creative director,
strategy guy,
blogger,
Canadian,

Christian,
speeder,
writer,
social media guru…
and the list keeps growing.

In the blank space to the right of my list, take the time to write down the things you've been known for. (Can you come up with a longer list than mine?) Life has allowed or propelled us to be known for all of these things.

Now, let's discover together how we can control the list so what we're known for can give us a way to break through into this world and, while we're going, have greater influence so people everywhere will listen to our gospel message, join this wonderful community through baptism, and enjoy the fellowship offered through obedience (Matt. 16:19-20). Let's discover a *thread* of communication that unites our ministries and gives us a strategy for pursuing our world.

I pray that, in a small way, this simple book will be used to help grow the Church… my community, my passion, and my client.

Part I

BE READY

I

CHOICES

We are our choices.

—J. P. SARTRE

There are some churches who break through in their communities. Everything they do seems to grab the attention of those around them. Their churches swell in numbers, so other ministries start copying them, hoping for success in their local communities. Honestly, most don't experience the success. Some are outright failures at duplicating the ministries.

What causes the success in a growing church?

I know that God empowers it. He's said that His Church will prevail.

So why do thousands of churches fail annually while our communities have lost interest in our ministries? Perhaps, there's a *thread* we can discover so that we can reconnect with our local community where God has planted us… a *thread* that God will use to grow His Church and your ministry.

There is. So let's discover it.

The Problem

People have so many choices to be made. They must choose the way they fill their time every day and especially on Sundays: to attend church, spend time with family, or choose to sleep later on Sunday mornings. Sadly, church is quickly being ignored since more of our population isn't connected to a place of worship!

Churches are disappearing.

The community has moved away from its need of church. Did you know that almost 4,000 churches close their doors each year in America? The sad thing? Most Christians have no idea that this is happening.

But it's not just entire churches that are disappearing. A large demographic study conducted by churchleaders.com tracked 250,000+ orthodox Christian churches, as well as the findings of barna.com studies, show a steady decline in church attendance over the last couple of decades. It's estimated that 3,500 people are leaving the local church in America... every single day!

These sobering numbers are a sure sign that the church needs to become known for something different. Otherwise, we're risking continued decline.

Church, we need to wake up.

The Millennials (who reached adulthood around 2000) are being studied by Barna and others as the important next-generation group who doesn't understand the need for church. In fact, Barna's research shows that 43% of the Millennials who are currently established in our churches will drop out in the next decade. That overall community—which boasts 80% of those who don't regularly attend a church on a regular basis—don't understand the value of going to church because they don't truly "know" it. And now, sadly, almost half the youth who do "know" the church—because they were raised in a Bible-believing congregation—are going to leave it.

The church has lost its way, especially regarding how we're known. And if we're not known for anything relevant, we'll have further declines.

Let's stop this from happening. Let's acknowledge change and embrace it.

Know what choices to control.

You can't make choices for your community and congregation! So let me show you that its about controlling *our* choices in our ministries so that they'll want to choose (or consider choosing) our church ministries.

You'll quickly see that intentionally being known for something revitalizes your church's reputation and informs your community about the benefits you have for them. You'll break through into their lives and reconnect quickly with them.

Let's control our choices (with God's direction) so that at the end of our days we won't lament that life seemed to choose our paths. God wants you to be known for seeking His will and reaching your community as effectively as possible. Either you'll establish your ministry's reputation (with God's direction), or life will run you. I want the first one! But I have to admit it wasn't always that way.

Life's choices happened to me.

I landed my first branding agency job in the mid-1980s. I found myself—what felt like for the first time—making my own decisions. During pre-school, my parents, of course, made most of my decisions. Throughout elementary and middle school, my teachers and parents shared the bulk of decision-making power in my life. And then for my Christian high school years, I again felt like all decisions were being made for me. When I chose to go to a very conservative, Bible-believing college in the Southern United

States, it was a huge decision to leave Eastern Canada although I really don't remember how I made the decision. Thinking back, it just seemed to have happened. My parents didn't push me like parents would these days. I just remember thinking that I wanted to go to a Christian university and study graphic design, communication, drama, and music. It seemed almost impossible that I could find all of that in one college.

A girl I was dating at the time told me her brother was at a place 1400 miles away that sounded like what I desired. Knowing very little of the school and having only ventured as far south as New Hampshire at the time, my parents drove me to South Carolina to a school I'd never visited before, in a state I'd only heard of, and a place where I knew only one other person on campus.

After I unloaded my two suitcases of clothes and a box of books and trinkets, I said to my parents, "Well, I guess that's it. Thank you for driving me here. I'll see you at Christmas." I retreated to my dorm room as they drove off campus.

The next time my parents would visit campus again was my senior year when I graduated with my degree. Even though they weren't near me while I studied, I was allowed to call once a month to talk for just a few minutes. They didn't make many decisions for me, but the college gladly took that role.

After four years, armed with my diploma, I returned to Canada. I felt free. I was entering a new stage of life. I would make all of my own decisions.

Then, life happened. I got a dream advertising agency job, met my soon-to-be wife, became a deacon in a vibrant Baptist church, had kids, bought houses, changed jobs, and the list rattles on. Sure, I was making decisions, but looking back, it felt like I was reacting to external influences more than proactively deciding anything.

Does that sound like you?

Too many people "fall into a life." Outside reasons seem to prowl, identifying those who aren't in control (or are on a cliff of uncertainty) and push us over the brink. You may land on your feet or discover a great life from the push. But often, we later feel regret.

Let's break the cycle.

"It's not about time, it's about choices.
How are you spending your choices?"
— *Beverly Adamo*

Agency life is full of constant pressure from clients who want something moments after they request it. And they know exactly what they want, can't produce it themselves, and demand creativity in achieving what they think is right. There are so many choices in each of the details of each step. But agencies are structured in such a way that our clients often decide what is right and wrong.

Don't get me wrong; I love the agency world, most of my clients, and the work I've been privileged to be part of. But after more than 30 years of being client-led, I realized that I had allowed myself to become known for something. And it wasn't something I wanted to be known for. It had just happened to me. And although it was "good," I wanted to be part of the process of being known for something I felt was part of God's path. I didn't want to just be client-led.

Like many who are in ministry, you may feel the same way. Substitute "congregation" where I said "clients"; does that sum up your life? Do your congregation, opportunities, and external constraints seem to guide you?

Do you intentionally make choices in your church? Or do you *have* to make choices?

There's nothing worse than getting to the end of a day and feeling like you didn't intentionally do anything. There has to be a better way. I don't want to get to the end of my life and realize I didn't control at least some of the paths to my successes (with God's guidance, of course).

My Breakthrough

One day as I was driving across the Lake Pontchartrain Causeway on the way to speak at a pastors' conference outside of New Orleans, I realized that what I'd been teaching my clients for many years was what I needed to *listen* to. What hit me like a brick was that life, with all of its efforts, is so limited. We don't have time, yet we need to take the time to use our time more effectively. But how can you do that in your Church? It comes down to making better communication choices to assist our community's decision-making into a quick process. This is important to understand because we want people to choose quickly what our church is offering.

The Pastors I was going to talk to needed to become known for something. Something so relevant and established, that their communities would quickly choose them—even if they weren't necessarily looking for "church".

But before we decide what a church should be known for, let's understand why and how a person in your community makes decisions quickly.

Your audience makes fast choices.

Few people are able to make confident decisions without the research required to feel fully in control. So, because time is of the essence, they make choices based on what they know or *feel* about something. Here are the steps in this sequence:

1: People have a lot of choices to make.

It's possible that we make 5,000 choices during an average 16-hour day. That requires a decision every 11.5 seconds. There's no way we can make these decisions consciously. In fact, to prove the point, when we arrive at a website we make a lot of ultra-fast decisions. Within 1-2 seconds of arriving on a page, we choose to jump to another URL or to stay. Then, within 3-4 seconds, we decide where to click the first time.

This isn't just online though. In "real life," we make decisions quickly when someone approaches us. Do we nod, say "hi", reach out to shake hands, or simply ignore the person? The number of decisions required in a day isn't decreasing; it's increasing. So our speed to a decision needs to increase as well.

2: You'd think we make decisions logically. But, we don't.

Think about the last time you sat at a restaurant, staring at a menu. You know you need to eat nutritious foods, and perhaps, you've gained a few pounds. You glance at the low-calorie items, and some even sound good. Then, you glance at the fried platter of goodness that's pictured for your convenience. You logically know which decision you should make, but you choose to do what feels good emotionally.

Or, maybe you're halfway through a meal and really aren't hungry anymore, yet you still keep eating. It's not logical. Our decisions usually will fault toward the emotional rather than the logical. It's why most women (usually the more emotional gender?) tend to make the most purchasing decisions in a relationship.

3: We make decisions based on what we already know about something.

Because we're required to make quick choices, we make most of our decisions based on a foundation of what we already know. If someone was to say, "Hey, let's do lunch," you have to decide on a quick "yes" or "no" answer. But we all know the tension that fills the room when someone asks, "So, where should we go?" The problem arises because it forces us to understand all the parts of the equation; and there's lots we don't know like "What do I want to eat right now?" and "What does the other person like or not like?" Trying to balance wanting to make the decision quickly while not wanting to look like an impulsive jerk who doesn't think about others, we resist the decision.

But if someone says, "I'd love to do Mexican food. Want to come? Where would you suggest?", it starts to limit the decisions and introduces things you do know. If they add, "But I don't have too much time", you instantly can narrow down the choices. You may be doomed to a Taco Bell entree. Or you may just have to make up an excuse that keeps you from eating another Crunch Wrap Supreme.

4. We want our choices to solve something.

We want our choices to fulfill a perceived need or, even more rudimentary, an actual pain that has surfaced. "I'm hungry" tells your brain that you need to make a choice of what you'll eat to satisfy your hunger... or if you'll choose not to eat right now. Of course, this is merely postponing the decision to find a solution. Most choices rise to importance based on how prevalent or intense the pain is. If you just burned yourself on the stove, you quickly choose to remove your hand. If you don't have a lot of time when you're hungry or you're driving by the only fast food restaurant around, you stop and eat.

Okay, enough about food because it's making me hungry. And anyone who knows me realizes I eat my main meal only so I can finally eat dessert (to me, that's logical *and* emotional).

Summary

Our audience wants the time to weigh all the pros and cons but they don't have enough time to figure out all the details in your church.

So, here's the crux. Ultimately, in order to influence a community, we need them to quickly choose us for something (a thread). We need to become known for being the solution to something that's predominant in their lives.

Be known for something.

It's the fastest way to reconnect and influence your community so they'll choose your church, your ministry. It's about revitalizing your church's reputation with something biblical, authentic, and desired.

At the end of each chapter, I've provided some questions for small group discussion to make sure you and your team have processed the chapter, knowing how it relates to each of you and helps you to progress down the path to being known for something. Enjoy the ride!

Discussion #1

Is there obvious decline or stagnation in our ministries? What do we base this on? What are the measurable categories we should be watching?

Have we lost a connection with our community? Or even our congregation?

If the following statements describe us, explain how:

"I sometimes feel like I'm a boat on the water with the currents pushing me."

"I feel like a fish who can swim upstream and face even the toughest currents."

"I want to reconnect with my community God's placed me in so I can influence better!"

Are we willing to make some difficult choices to reconnect?

Want additional information, downloads, and worksheets? Join us at www.beknownbook.com.

2
PERCEPTION VS. REALITY

Life isn't about finding yourself.
Life is about creating yourself.

— George Bernard Shaw

Has it occurred to you that your church is currently "known for something"? In fact we all are. It's a way to categorize people, places and things so we can choose them (or reject them) quickly for various reasons. It's a sobering thought. I've had opportunities to talk with high school classes about personal branding and to encourage them as they consider their lives. Before speaking to them, I'll ask a teacher about one of the students I point out. The teacher usually tells me a quick summary of the student's life.

"He struggles because of a bad family situation."

"She's a go-getter who'll have all the right answers."

"He really tries hard but has a learning disability that holds him back."

How would you have been described if I asked your high school teacher to describe you? Would it have been accurate? Would you have wanted to change that perception?

What about in college?

More relevantly, what would your co-workers say about you now? Or the people who follow you on Facebook, Twitter, Snapchat, or Instagram?

What my social media feeds reveal is a lot of Christians who complain, attack, and associate with the wrong people. I'm sure you have either hidden certain people or simply choose to ignore those who are known for things you don't agree with.

Being known for something is hard to control. But if we don't control it, the people around us will control it for us. And that's called perception. In other words, *who you are* is not necessarily *what you're known for*. But what you're known for becomes people's *perception* of who you are.

Your church is known for something. You may not like it. Or you may embrace it wholly. It may be based in fact or it may be perception. No matter, perception becomes reality.

Perception is your brand.

In 2000, my family and I moved to North Carolina from New Brunswick, Canada. We came so I could start my progression toward helping churches. I worked a bit with churches in Atlantic Canada, but compared to the Southern United States, the ability to set up a branding agency for churches in Canada was quite difficult because we didn't have nearly as many churches as the South. North Carolina has almost 4,000 Southern Baptist Churches alone, perhaps as many churches as all denominations combined in the entire Maritime Provinces. It made sense that, if I wanted to be known for working with churches, I should move to where a lot of churches are located. Granted, now, the internet is making it easier to impact an audience even if you're not close in proximity to them.

We started attending a large, vibrant church when we arrived. I sang in the choir and praise team, sang an occasional solo, and was also a drama lead from time to time. I was usually introduced as "the Canadian," so many thought they knew who I was. I found it difficult to know people truly because they felt they already knew me. Perception will often keep someone from really knowing someone.

There was someone in our church I knew about. Well, I knew some things about him that helped me to form my opinion of him. People thought we looked alike, and a few people asked if he was my brother. After I narrated a patriotic musical, many described him to me as "a guy who's the voice of the Wake Forest Demon Deacons" that has a great speaking voice, too. I remember the first time someone pointed him out to me. I was at a local restaurant (go figure), and he was doing a live remote for his sports show. The person I was eating with said, "Oh, there's Stan," as though I certainly would know him. I didn't. My friend said, "He's the voice of the Deacons." I basically knew him as the "sports guy" with the rich voice in our church.

Fast forward a decade, Stan and I still never had met formally. He had been on my radar, but I never actually had crossed paths with him. We have a big church with multiple locations and services!

I had agreed to teach a new Adult Bible Fellowship Class (what our church calls Sunday school) a few years ago. We'd taught younger classes before, but I had never thought I was able to teach people my own age. It was intimidating. And because I envisioned myself as a decade younger than my actual age, I felt that 50-year-olds were ancient.

The first day of class arrived, and my wife and I had been praying that we'd have more than two attend the class. Several couples we didn't know walked in, and as the class filled up, my nervousness grew, too.

Then, Stan walked in. He's one of those guys whose stature screams sports like he's a football hero. It took me a couple of weeks to gain the courage even to speak to him although he sat in our growing class. All I could eek out was, "So you're the 'voice of Wake Forest sports', right?" It was what he was known for.

I should state for the record that I'm not a sports guy. I will never be known for sports, my knowledge of sports, or even how to cheer effectively for a sports team. Sports intimidates me. I'm literally scared of anyone who is wearing sports colors, jerseys, or uniforms because I may say something wildly stupid that will get my Canadian butt whooped... not because I mean any harm but because of ignorance.

Stan intimidated me.

He turned with a coffee in his hand and said, "I am. But the reason my wife and I came to this class is because your class isn't all about sports."

It was the beginning of a great friendship.

What I'd heard and been told (perception) became reality in my mind and kept me from a great relationship. I figured he would never want to talk with someone like me.

Perception is reality.

Likewise, the perception of church certainly keeps a community away from knowing it.

Perception *is* reality. To deny this is a huge problem. Often, I hear people say that their church is known for something that they don't believe they are. They'll need to change people's perception in order to change "reality."

Unfortunately, we've been taught to ignore perception. Most of our parents told us simply to ignore the mean kids because what they're saying is surely false. If that's a lifesaving mechanism for someone, it's a deceptive one. Even if someone is spreading lies about you or your church, you need to address them, especially if the lies take hold!

Branding is what people say about something (or someone) behind the leader's back.

Yes, it's difficult to discover others' perceptions. Often, what is said about you or your ministry when you're not around is almost impossible to find out. The easiest way is to ask true friends for their honest opinion, or your church should conduct a community focus group to discover it.

Discovering Perception

A focus group is a small selection of people who don't necessarily know each other but are connected to you or your organization somehow. Invite this group (often less than 10 people) to a location where they'll feel free to share and talk. We recommend a location not connected to your ministry. It's wise to have a facilitator who knows you well and wants your best interest. It's best not to use yourself or your church leadership because people may not share openly if they feel the facilitator is "one of you." You'll only hear what they think you want to hear rather than reality. Remember that the purpose of the focus group is to hear the honest truth. And sometimes, that hurts.

Questions should be asked in a conversational format, including preference questions and questions to seek understanding and perception of your category (church, charity, ministry, etc.). As the group's comfort level expands, narrow the questions to specific, targeted concerns. Sometimes, it's wise to have several group meetings with two or three different demographic groups to find out how widespread or targeted the perceptions are. We often offer a modest monetary compensation for their participation (or, at the least, a light meal or snack).

What I've found? People in a comfortable, safe conversation like to speak their minds. And from their minds come perceptions.

Remember again that we have been trained to ignore negative things. But those little inklings of bad stuff will sink a ship if left unfettered. Make sure the facilitator has total freedom in sharing his or her gut perception of the discussions. The goal is to unearth any possible misperceptions and to address them.

It's difficult to change perception.

Once you have the raw information in front of you, realize that it's hard to change perception. If it's totally wrong, try to discover how it was started, perpetuated, and what it means ultimately to your future. Remember that people often don't want to believe that they are totally wrong, so it will be better for you to start with what most believe and see if there's a way to reorient those misperceptions slowly. Of course, there are times when misperceptions need to be publicly addressed and cleared up quickly; don't ignore them!

Your mother was, of course, right. Often, the perception of who we are is based upon who our friends and associates are. Many people believe that they don't have control of this. And it's true that, as a church, you can't control the people who attend. And because the Church is made up of sinners, we have the same issue Jesus had when He got the bad rap of associating with sinners (Mark 2:13-17).

Rather than getting caught in the web of whose perceptions we can and can't control, let's take an inventory of the words, people, and groups with whom we are associated. Understanding this will allow us to control the perception of being associated with them and to change those perceptions.

Being a Church

Ultimately, whether we like it or not, our Christian groups are labeled as a "church," which means that we are associated with all other churches. I often hear pastors say, "We're not like other churches." The problem with that? The world perceives you as the same. If "church" is in your name, perception-wise, you are like all churches. And if you remove "church" from your name, while still meeting as a large group of believers with singing and sermons, you *are* a church. Walks like a duck... quacks like a duck... it's a duck. Realize it, and move forward, trying to change that perception (or, at least, living with that understanding).

There was a perception study done to discover generally-held perceptions of various Christian ideas. When the un-churched were asked about the relevance of Church congregations, a full one-third of the respondents had no idea how a congregation could be beneficial to them.

Historically, we've brought a lot of that negative perception on ourselves. Coupled with the Church being "salt" in a world decaying because of sin, we are rarely discussed in good terms, especially in the media. (Yes, salt stings! We'll deal with a solution for this.) But please realize that, as a Church, we're struggling to gain positive traction. We've ultimately done a great job of being salt and a poor job of being light. ✗

Perceptions of Jesus

What are the perceptions of Jesus? He even asked His disciples (like a small focus group), "Who do people say I am?" He then asked, "Who do *you* say I am?" (Mark 8:27-30; Matt. 16:13-20). As He walked the earth, people had misperceptions of who He was. And even His disciples weren't totally accurate, except for Peter, who blurted out, "You are the Messiah, the Son of the living God!" Jesus went on to say that, upon that huge declaration, God would build the Church. That's us! But then, He admonished His disciples not to tell anyone. Obviously, that was for the immediate purpose of allowing Him to remain alive until His time to be crucified. Jesus knew how to clear up perception: tell something truthful that makes sense to the audience, communicating it over and over at the right times.

Interestingly, a perception study was done about people's perceptions of Jesus. He got some great ratings from all around the world and from other religions. People ultimately love the idea of Jesus. As long as we have Him on our side, we have a solid foundation. Upon Him as the Rock, He'll build His Church. We may see a slide in local, "small-c" church attendance, but we can rest assured that the universal, "big-C" Church will never vanish.

Note: If you'd like a complete study on creating a healthy, Biblical local church, I'd recommend *Nine Marks of a Healthy Church* by Mark Dever.

Perceptions of Church Leaders

Who are your ministry leaders? What are people's perceptions of them in the church and outside of the church? Perceptions of those who are "in charge" are significant.

If you are a ministry leader, are you seen as holier-than-thou? One of the saved sinners? Have it all together? Authentic? These are issues that play into the greater perception of who your church is. You can control this perception!

Perceptions of Your Denomination

Your church is probably associated with a larger group of churches. Even independent churches are perceived as being part of the denomination called "independent." If you're part of a mainstream denomination—and you refer to that denomination in your church's name, constitution, or website—you need to deal with how your denomination is perceived.

Many of the largest denominations, no matter how great their charity and mission is, are perceived poorly by local communities. Yes, you probably can't change that, but you need to realize what the community's perception is when it comes to your name designation. Often, it's easy to be quick to associate with the perception *you* have of your denomination, but that won't help how you're perceived in the community.

At the same time, the comfort level increases for many people seeking a church with a denominational name. In fact, one of the first things people are looking for when browsing for a church online is your doctrinal affiliation and core beliefs. It appears that, for those who are aware of denominations, that a denominational name (e.g. Baptist, Methodist, Presbyterian, etc.) helps their comfort as such churches appear to be more "mainstream" and "normal."

If you don't have a denomination in your name, you need to explain clearly what your beliefs are, not as a formal doctrinal statement but as an easy-to-understand, "what we believe" section on your church website. The more you can demonstrate how those beliefs drive your actions, the better.

Perception is reality, so deal with it as reality. To understand what you need to be known for, you must understand where you are. If you've ever tried to use a map app to get directions, the first step is for the map to determine where you're currently located. If the app can't do that, it can't give you directions.

Identify where you are in the minds of your community. Then, seek direction.

OUR CHURCH FUNCTIONS IN A "COCOON" OF CHURCH + SCHOOL

Discussion #2

On a scale of 1 to 10 (1 = worthless, 10 = very successful), what is our community's general perception of our church?

If we were to use a service like Survey Monkey (to assure anonymity), what key groups in our church would you like to ask perception questions? What questions would we ask them? Here are some to start the list:

If someone was randomly asked in our community to name a great church, would we be on the list? Who else would be there? Why?

What do we do really well?

What do we do poorly and should improve upon?

What are we known for in the community?

What are we known for within our membership (people who know us)?

What are some things we can do in the next couple of weeks that will help us to understand how our church is perceived? (e.g. talk to key leaders, commission a mall survey, talk to the board about being known for something, etc.)

How can we be more about Jesus and less about the current perception of church?

What do *we* need to change or reinforce personally to help improve how our church is perceived?

Want additional information, downloads, and worksheets? Join us at www.beknownbook.com.

3

BE KNOWN FOR SOMETHING

Before we jump into the steps and specifics for how we revitalize a Church's reputation, let's take a quick look at what I mean that a church needs to be known for something.

In fact, there's a possibility that you're already known for the right thing and you simply need to learn how to communicate it better (we deal with that later in the book).

It takes quite a bit of self-reflection and soul-searching to realize whether you're currently known for the right thing or if you need to determine what the thread actually is.

Or like many church leaders who have gone through this process, you may have discovered that you've been communicating the wrong things.

Not a Vision or Mission Statement

Everything needs to spring from your church's core benefits. This is not your vision statement or mission statement. We struggle many times with churches who have spent months and months developing these wordy paragraphs that are their raison d'être (reason for being), and now, they believe it needs to be inscribed everywhere. And obviously, their benefits are presented essentially as their mission.

I spoke with a larger church recently whose leadership team was incredibly proud of their "mission." They had worked countless hours to compress their long mission statement into three shorter statements, something like "Gather. Grow. Go." It's a nice way to create something to allow an internal audience (the members and staff) to understand their purpose for ministry. But this isn't what you will become known for in a community. There's nothing in those three words that will attract an unbeliever or former church attendee to come to your church.

I had the opportunity to ask some of their members if they knew what their church was known for, and I got honest answers like...

- "We're a really big church."
- "We've got a bunch of locations."
- "One church, many locations."
- "The church that causes traffic problems on Sunday morning."
- And then, there were a couple of people who said something like, "Oh, it's that thing that the pastor keeps repeating... the 'Gather, Ggggg...,' and Ggggg...' slogan."

Yep, if your members can't remember it, the community certainly won't hear about it. Perhaps, these phrases are a waste of time. Or (trying to be more positive) maybe it's an internal slogan that's useful for the core team. I'm not saying you shouldn't have a mission statement, but it should only be used to provide internal motivation to produce the audience's benefit. It's the course-correction guide. It's what drives you to produce and achieve. It's internal speak rather than for external communications.

Imagine that you're very hungry, and you'd like to have a great chicken sandwich. You spot a Chick-fil-A, pull into the parking lot, jump out of your car, and proceed to the entrance. You pull open the door, and the aromas make you anticipate the chicken sandwich even more. Nevertheless, the manager stops you and starts to explain his business plan and the reason his staff cooks amazing food. You interrupt him and say, "But I just want a chicken sandwich." Ignoring your comment, he continues to share the importance of his mission. You want a chicken sandwich.

Instead of giving to *you* what *you* want, he's telling you why *he* wants to do what *he* does. He's keeping you from getting what you're looking for.

Local churches have communities who need something that we have (Jesus), but we're adding a barrier of internal mission talk that stands in the way of what they're looking for. The problem is they don't know what we have for them. Our internal talk, at best, only attracts people from other churches while turning off the unchurched.

Rarely does a mission statement ever lead to a "sale" (or bring in a family or individual into a church). The mission statement should only lead and guide your internal operations. It's the recipe to a great product, and your benefit is the outcome of experiencing the product.

A chef may have a mission statement to produce the best wholesome, home-grown, antibiotic-free bakery items so that she can wholeheartedly support local organic farms while producing world-class pastries. But the benefit for the person eating them is likely that he or she enjoys French pastries made from the best-quality ingredients, a decadent treat that can be eaten with peace of mind.

With the local church, we have something else going on. We're "converting" someone to change their thinking and actions through the power of the gospel. A church's mission statement explains the reasons that the people in the congregation are doing what they're doing, but it ultimately has nothing to do with the person who is attracted to the ministry for another reason.

A mission statement doesn't give a reason for them to attend. An unconverted community member is not going to want to "win the world for Jesus Christ" as many mission statements insist. It's simply an excellent impetus for those within the congregation to do what they do. We must stop leading with our internal messaging.

The benefit for someone who has no faith in Christ to attend a church might be to help the person's kids get moral training, to get hope in a world that doesn't make sense, or to get help for his or her struggling marriage.

Mission statements reassure an organization that they're on track at a DNA level while communicated benefits ensure that the organization will actually exist in the future!

It's all about benefits.

I have known many organizations that had awesome mission statements yet failed, but an organization with well-communicated benefits—that is, the benefits are unique, valuable, and needed solutions—will rarely fail. It's a huge claim, but the definition of a benefit is that it's desired. Communicate it properly, and you will succeed.

You need to be known for something, and that "something" is one of your prominent benefits.

Requirements for Your Thread

Think you know what it is now? It's possible. Feel free to write your thoughts in the book as we walk through the process. You're ultimately trying to create a tagline (a thread) that summarizes why people need to engage with your church. This is a brand-positioning statement, and here's the criteria to weigh your ideas and create a successful "be known for something" communication thread:

It needs to be simple.

This short statement (1-5 words) you're creating doesn't need to be a sentence, but it can contain a period, creating a sentence fragment. It needs to be a simple concept that people will embrace and remember. The best ones have one simple thread.

It needs to be somewhat "open" in thought.

Ambiguous. The more specific the statement is, the harder it will be to "roll it out" across your ministry. Consider having several meanings as it will be used across various audiences, but make sure it could never take on a negative meaning.

It needs to be emotionally-charged.

The more emotionally-charged a statement is, the better. Consider the emotion someone will have when he or she experiences the benefit. Happy? Delighted? Relieved? Content? Make sure this emotion is the feeling you or your church exudes. If happiness is your emotion, question whether your foyer and ministry areas create happy environments.

It needs to be benefit-driven.

The statement should refer to a solution and, therefore, a prominent pain... or, a path to a goal. That's why you'll do some exercises to get to this stage.

It needs to feel like your congregation.

Be Biblical, genuine, authentic, and real. You don't want this to be established for the sake of change. However, it can be aspirational; although, this should only be done with extreme caution.

You can choose something that may be a bit obscure but incredibly needed in the community, and with a slight push and reinforcement, your congregation can become known for it. This takes more intentionality, encouragement, and motivation. I've seen it work incredibly well with churches over the years. The "be known for something" statement shouldn't be a hard-sell though. If you think you really need to sell it a lot (with skepticism as the initial reaction), you're pursuing the wrong thread.

It needs to be unique.

Do a quick search online for what churches in your area are using as taglines and communication messages. Then, broaden your search to look for what secular businesses are doing that are offering similar benefits. The more unique you are in the communication thread, the easier it will be for you to break through with it. If someone else is already known for something in your area, and you say you want to be known for that as well, you'll always be a copycat. The first *to* market with a concept usually becomes first *in* market.

The Be-Known-For-Something Thread

A be-known-for-something thread consists of the following elements:

Be

The declaration of who and what you are. To *be* something, you have to practice it consistently and perfect it in all aspects of your organization. If you're known for being an uplifting congregation, people close to you see your church exhibiting motivation and encouragement. Being something is difficult to achieve. It takes a consistent effort and reinforcement of the concept. Verbalizing it increases its strength, but the concept doesn't require convincing in order for people to believe it. You either are, or you're not.

Known

Known requires promotion, marketing, and advertising. You can "be" something, but it must be told or communicated effectively in order to be known. This is the end goal. *Known* requires a concept that can be remembered easily. A solution to a pain and a path to a goal are the easiest concepts for your audience to remember.

For

Often, churches are known more for what they're against than for what they are *for*. If properly worded, unique, and benefit-driven, a good be-known-for-something thread can overcome a negative aura. People will want to join your positive movement as your thread will overshadow any negativity.

Something

Not many things. One compelling thing is easiest to remember. Resist the urge to choose the three things for people to remember (the "_____. _____. _____." motto approach). If you tell a group of people to remember one thing and emphasize it (e.g. "I want you all to remember the word, 'chocolate.' I love chocolate, and 89 percent of Americans love it, too. Remember chocolate!"), the next time you stand in front of that group and ask "what word did I tell you to remember?", the audience will be more apt to remember it. If you tell them to remember two words, fewer will remember both words. If you tell them to remember three words, they'll be one-third third less likely to remember them. Short-term memory is said to max out at seven words. Get your thread embedded into people's long-term memory. A one-word concept will be remembered the longest.

Simple. Right? Nope. Even after almost three decades of doing these exercises, I find it challenging. But that's what makes it fun. Just remember that you're committing to this be-known-for-something thread for *years*. Not months. If it's working for you, you've become known for it, and it's still a solution to a prominent pain or path to a goal in your community, keep it for another three to five years. If it starts to lose its attractive power, consider strengthening how you're using and promoting it before you consider changing it.

This is NOT a sermon series.

This is a DNA scarlet thread that is woven within everything you're doing. It's so important that I would recommend trade-marking it and purchasing the URL (point the domain to your main church website domain). Then, check its traction by checking the thread's URL analytics compared to your main church URL.

We have found that people are more apt to remember what a church is known for than the actual church's name. How many times have you asked, "What's that restaurant where everyone yells a welcome when you enter?" Isn't it perfect that Moe's Southwest Grill added their name to what they became known for! "Welcome to Moe's" helps you remember that they love you and want you to feel welcome, *and* it reminds you of their name. They also own WelcomeToMoes.com and Moes.com. Moe's is actually an acronym for "Musicians, Outlaws, and Entertainers." Most people refer to the restaurant as Moe's without realizing the actual name is Moe's Southwestern Grill.

Names aren't as important as people remembering your thread because the thread contains the benefit to them. That's also why you must ensure good search engine optimization so you can be discovered by your thread, too.

I started PinPoint Creative Group (PinPointCreative.com)—a traditional marketing, branding, and design agency for the church—in 2000 and created the brand positioning "Be Known For Something" for PinPoint in 2010. I bought the URL for BeKnownForSomething.com and started communicating the concept. Within a year, it was generating almost five times the unique visitors to our website, and we're now receiving almost 10 times more visitors to BeKnownForSomething.com than PinPointCreative.com. When the idea, benefit, and solution resonates, you know it works. We've actually stopped communicating our original name now altogether, and the URL just points to our main BeKnownForSomething.com domain.

I may have gotten ahead of a few things in this chapter, but I wanted to establish what we're aiming for. Now, let me take a few steps backwards and explain the essential steps we recommend so you can discover what your church should be known for.

But first, let me address an elephant in the room.

Discussion #3

Does our mission statement attract non-church people in our community?

If we're "being" our mission statement; what benefit would speak directly to someone in our community?

Are we like most churches? Are we more "for" something or more "against" things?

What's the biggest benefit for attending our church? What would the average regular attender say it is?

If there's more than one thing, do we think we could decide on *the* thing? The answer we want to hear regularly to this question, "so why do you attend this church?". Would the answer encourage (or entice) someone else who doesn't attend a church now to attend?

Does the leadership of the church like to change the "theme" too frequently? So often that nothing "sticks"? If yes, why do we think they do that?

Want additional information, downloads, and worksheets? Join us at www.beknownbook.com.

4

CREATE AN ATTITUDE OF CHANGE

*The only person who is educated is the one who
has learned how to learn and change.*

—CARL ROGERS, AMERICAN PSYCHOLOGIST

What if, during this process of discovery, you realize there's a greater issue than just deciding what you should be known for? What if you hear from multiple sources that there's a good reason your church isn't growing. Perhaps you're stuck in a rut.

Of course, ruts *can* be good because they're essentially another name for being known for something. Maybe you like your sweater vests. Or maybe you can't drink anything other than Starbucks coffee. We all have deep grooves that we find ourselves in. Even people who like to change also have protected areas that they'd never consider changing.

I'm not the regular grocery shopper in our house. My wife, Tammy, does a great job of watching our cupboards and refrigerator, noticing what we're getting low on, and replenishing our essentials from the local stores.

Recently, I offered to pick up a few things at the local grocery store. I couldn't believe how many choices there were on the shelves! I was there to buy that pre-mixed squirting stuff that allows you to flavor your own water. Mio was the brand I had been using, so I was going to buy that because I liked their light lemonade flavor. I made my way toward the Kool-Aid section, figuring I'd find it tucked in with the Crystal Light or other flavor crystals. Much to my surprise, I found an entire section dedicated to the little squeeze containers. Who knew? I thought my biggest decision was going to be about flavor, but I discovered there were at least 40 choices between brands and flavors. There were also in-store coupons that swayed me from my Mio lemonade for which I had come. I ended up leaving the store with five different lemon-flavored liquids.

For a world that doesn't love change, this proves we sure want a lot of choices.

Marketing communications is simply about convincing people that they may want to try something different than what they usually experience or use regularly. It's about getting someone out of a rut.

When I travel to help churches, I'm often in areas where I've never been before, so I try to eat at restaurants we don't have near our home. I love "different." I should confess that I'm not like most people because I really do love change and experiencing new things. Maybe you figured that out when I filled our cupboards with different lemonade-flavored squirt containers. (By the way, I like the Minute Maid lemonade flavor best right now, in case you were wondering.)

Perhaps I'm being far too transparent when I tell you that I often will sit in my home or office and change the furniture arrangements, just so I can enjoy the change. It's probably the underlying urge that lies within me to renovate homes. For me, there's nothing like walking through an old room and envisioning what it "could" look like. I love to dream big. I try not to allow the squelching nature of a budget to cramp my style. I research, sketch, and browse through Lowes or Home Depot. Usually, this occurs weeks and sometimes months before the renovation. I think about how great the before-and-after pictures will look and how much more pleasant the room will be. And then, I start selling the benefits to Tammy.

And as much as I love to change, I occasionally find myself not willing to change. It seems like a conflict. I understand why people battle with it. With so many changes possible, it's a constant battle to keep up with everything. My response can easily be to stay with what I have and to pretend I don't need to change.

It's ultimately a choice whether we change or get overwhelmed by the choices and choose to remain the same.

Does your church *need* to change?

It's a complex question. My father was the proverbial aging guy who—after a life of learning electronics, telephony, and computers—decided he couldn't keep up with how to set the time on his VCR. (For young people reading, this was the precursor to a DVR.) When we used to visit him (he passed away a few years ago), his VCR clock was always blinking on the pre-programmed 12:00. I couldn't understand why he didn't know the simple menu-driven process that would allow him to set the time.

Fast forward (no pun intended) to me sitting with one of my young-adult sons. He was explaining Minecraft or the latest gaming system upgrades. And I was fogging over. I had always wondered when I would meet my "flashing VCR light" moment. And remember I like to change!

Age is certainly a factor in all of this. I was more willing to change as a younger man than I am now. It pains me to write this.

Why? Because the implications of not having an attitude of change are huge.

What about you? As a ministry leader, do you want to keep your church the same? Do you struggle with the concept of change? Here's what it suggests if you don't want to change things around you...

It implies you're perfect.

It doesn't take much soul-searching to realize that I'm a flawed character. Anyone who follows my blog or social media channels knows that it's important for me to be transparent, honest, and critical of myself. By doing that, I realize that the list of things requiring change keeps growing. And then, I add the optional things (like home renovations) that seem to get more attention than the other things on the list. If you say you don't need to change, you're implying you don't need it. That's a huge problem. Think your church doesn't need to change? Is it perfect then?

It implies you're accepting status quo.

This is similar to the "perfection" declaration. But for those who say they're certainly not perfect but then say they don't want to change, they are actually saying they're accepting where they are in life. Their outcomes are what they'll accept. Or they've looked at the things they control and have convinced themselves that there are no better options out there. Do you accept the current state of your church?

It implies you don't have time to improve.

I've talked with many people about my incessant need to change, and their immediate reaction often is, "I don't know where you find the time!" Time has become the biggest barrier to improvement. People declare that they "don't have the time to do social media right," "overhaul their processes," "manage their teams properly," "have devotional times," etc. Don't allow time to keep you from needed change. The time will often be rewarded back to you in the same way that wise investments bring huge dividends. Are you willing to invest the time required to change your church ministries?

It implies it's not worth the effort.

If I told you that you can make tens of thousands of dollars if you learn how to do most of the work on your house renovations, many (or should that be most) will reply, "It's too much work." I'm amazed how many people won't even try to paint a room themselves. Excuses include "no time," "costs too much," or "it's not worth the effort." Each of these certainly have to be weighed. But many don't attempt something because they don't want to change, and many simply say it's not worth it.

Most changes required in the church are free and fairly easy. Effort is subjective. I'd rather fail than die without attempting. Many things that take our time and money are far less productive than things we should be doing. Keep reminding yourself of that!

Fears often keep us from changes.

The first time I tackled a simple plumbing job in our house (which I would not recommend for the faint-of-heart), I talked to a few people who had done it before, consulted a "pro" at the home improvement store, and watched some YouTube videos. Then, I felt ready. I figured that replacing a copper pipe and soldering it together couldn't really be that difficult. I turned the water off, made my cuts, put everything back together, and tried desperately to get the solder to retreat into the seam like everyone said it would. I heated the pipe, reheated it, stopped, watched the videos again, and then tried again. Then, I had convinced myself that the soldering had, in fact, worked although it didn't look like it was supposed to.

Tammy and my sons often help with projects, but when frustration sets in and the air turns dense, they often retreat to a safer area of the house. I called to Tammy to turn the master water faucet back on. It was located in another part of the house. Moments later, I found out that, when the pipe connector has the full force of water on it and it breaks apart, a person's hands cannot contain the spray that will soak someone in a matter of minutes. After the initial panic washed over me (pun intended) for what seemed like a long time, my yells got the water cut off again. Several attempts later, I gave up in defeat.

Because most of the renovations in our house occur on Saturdays, we went to bed that night, knowing that we had no water for showers before church in the morning. I don't remember much discussion when we all went to our rooms that night.

Why do I tell you such a story? I want you to realize that failure should not keep you from change. But it should give you pause before attempting it.

If you change nothing, nothing will change. So why don't ministry leaders like to change ministries around the church? The church has become known for staying the same.

Why change doesn't happen

1: Fear of Failure

Yes, people would rather live in failure than risk failing at an attempt to get better. I've done plumbing since that horrible weekend (referred to as "the plumbing disaster"). But if it involves soldering, I (reluctantly) call a plumber. (Well, actually, Tammy calls one for me.)

2: Fear of the Learning Curve

Remember when you finished high school or college, and you erroneously thought your learning was over? We all know it's never over. Part of having an attitude of change is having an attitude of learning. Improving. Many times, the learning curve is easier than it seems. Other times, it's not (should I mention soldering here?). But you'll never know until you try. But don't give up too early.

3: Fear of the Treadmill

As I try to keep up with technology, I often feel like someone who approaches the cardio area at a gym for the first time when the gym owner crazily decides to set all the treadmills at 10 miles per hour. I feel like the world is already running at a fast speed, and I'm just jumping on. Or when I'm finally adjusted to the speed of the treadmill and need to take a break, I feel like I'd be flung off the back because it's not stopping.

Once you adopt an attitude of change and actually start changing, you'll find that it's an ongoing, crazy environment that won't slow down. I would caution you to identify the speed you feel comfortable with and progress at that rate, remaining conscious of warning signs.

Worrying will never change the outcome.

Personally, I need constant change. As I study successful businesses, churches, and organizations, I have noticed that they almost always have an environment of change. I'm not saying that we must change *everything*. We all need principles that will not change because they're based on truth. And what is truth? Too many people declare truth and then watch it fail. Real truth doesn't fail. So, the only truth I know of is God's Word, the Bible.

Once we have those unchangeable principles established, how can we create a healthy environment where change can occur?

Decide to have an environment of change.

It's motivating to make the resolution internally, but saying it out loud to co-workers is even better. Half the battle is deciding you're not going to do things "just because we always have." Let's break that perception of the local church!

Know your limits.

How far will you go? How much change will you allow? Do you have a "test" to measure the change you'll pursue? These are valuable discussions to have.

Commit to preparation time.

Once the atmosphere for change is "allowed," take the time to prepare, research, and bring the necessary people up to speed *before* the change actually happens. If you don't, you may find that you'll leave many people behind, bewildered, and angry.

Understand your weaknesses.

The changes required are proportionate to the weaknesses in your organization. Make sure you clearly define those weaknesses and which ones need correction. It's okay not to solve everything! Prioritize.

Research the choices.

Want change? What kind of change? What products and services are available to help? You'll be amazed at the choices. Google, a consultant, and/or co-workers can help with this.

Weigh the costs.

Know the desired outcomes and limitations (time, budget, etc.) before you set out on this search. Remember that a cost is anything that consumes a limited resource. Time is a cost as it's not unlimited. Volunteers are costly even though they are "free" to your organization.

Get assistance or accountability.

You can't do it alone. Repeat that over and over until you get tired of saying it to yourself. Leaders often feel that the only way to do something properly is to do it themselves. That's why some leaders don't get a lot done. If you're doing something that someone on your team can be doing, you're doing a disservice to your organization. Delegate more.

Plot the benefits.

Change is difficult. You *will* need encouragement along the way. When I do a home improvement project, I always take "before" pictures so I can refer to them for motivation.

What are the benefits of change for your organization? Perhaps it's a graph of results, sharing weekly victorious stories, or regularly encouraging those on your team with words of affirmation.

Word of Caution

Be careful. There must be a proper balance with change. We've all worked with (or you're married to) someone who's not content with anything, so they constantly go through rounds and rounds of changes.

Some churches are trying to be like another church they've read about, so they have wild creativity meetings to try and gain that success for themselves. What ends up happening? They get negative results because change for the sake of change is bad.

Every service or product has a life cycle. It's rare that a successful product starts out with an instant "win" and maintains it. There's a natural bell curve that occurs throughout its life cycle. And it takes a lot of hard work, especially on the left side of the bell curve, when you're becoming known.

TV shows often have similar things occur. It takes some time for a show to pick up viewers, and then, the popularity is discussed around the water coolers, in classrooms, and on social media around the country. There's a huge increase in people who want to tune in. And they do, expecting greatness.

When a product or TV show has attracted the most attention that they'll ever attract, it's often because they start to run out of ideas for improving the product or show. A decline starts—or, at least, a flattening of the bell curve—and the writers or manufacturers lose their minds with wild ideas they'll attempt to correct the decline.

What once was known for amazing creativity now turns into a disconnect with over-the-top, pie-in-the-sky, wild thinking. This has been called "jumping the shark." It's that moment when everyone starts seeing the decline in quality, and the show takes on a corniness that is a feeble attempt at attracting more people.

If you're my age, you may remember that horrible episode of *Happy Days*. After four amazing seasons of popularity, some crazy writer trying to top the previous seasons has Fonzie (a key character) jumping over a shark while he water skis, and the decline of the show continued until it was gone.

Sometimes, gimmicks work to attract a big crowd... until you "jump a shark."

How about your church? Hopefully, you're tracking your attendance on a church communications calendar. How would you know if you're jumping a shark? Here are four ways to know if you're "jumping a shark":

1: Consider your "success."

Do you truly know the Biblical reasons for being who you are? Do you know the benefits you're offering to your community... what you're known for? It's critical to know what's caused your success, why people are attracted to you, and what keeps them there.

2: Know your bell curve.

You should be tracking your attendance. Are you growing, plateauing (the awkward flattening stage before decline), or declining? Most shark-jumping happens during a plateau or decline.

3. Understand innovation.

Measure how creative you've been in the past. Give it a score between 1 and 10. If you're a 3, don't try something that's a 9, especially if it feels like desperation to attract more people. Make sure all creativity and innovation is measured for consistency with the Bible and what you're known for.

4. Implement a quality control mechanism.

This is critical. Make sure that quality is the ultimate judge for things you try. If in doubt, don't.

We're called to go into the highways and byways and to compel people to come in. That can be done, but don't get (or look) desperate in that process. We're called to excellence and a higher standard in the Church. Make sure you have a process that allows for it. We need change but not too much wild change.

Discussion #4

On a scale of 1 to 10 (1 = not wanting to, 10 = desiring change all the time), where would we consider the leadership of our church when it comes to "wanting to change"? How about our church as a whole? Explain.

Would we like to change more, the same, or less?

What needs to change soon? What can be a goal date for accomplishing these changes?

What are things at our church that will never change (or should never change)? (Remember that being known for something involves a thread of consistency in various areas, so some things shouldn't change.)

Want additional information, downloads, and worksheets? Join us at www.beknownbook.com.

Part 2

BE CONSISTENT

5

BEING KNOWN FOR SOMETHING

I am known currently for

_____.

I want to be known for

_____.

Everyone makes choices because change is inevitable. We simply need to be known for something so people can embrace us. And by doing so, we'll influence them. Does that mean we'll need to change things? Possibly. But it's about being authentic to who you are.

We must become known for the right things to influence those around us. Why?

Because our world has a ton of choices, our community relies heavily on what they already know about something before making a decision. They compartmentalize people, things, organizations, and virtually everything else into what they know about them generally. These generalizations become key.

The search engines—Google, Yahoo, and Bing—do the same kind of thing. They go through every web page in the entire world and figure out (according to their algorithms) what people might need that information for. That's the only way they can deliver the results as quickly as they do when we search online for something.

For most of us, our compartmentalizing is more about perception than reality. We pick up a "sense" about something, and we subconsciously consider it as fact.

So how can we intentionally become known for something when the target is established within the individual minds of each person in our community? It's not as complicated as you'd think. But first, we need to realize a basic truth:

People love to "make up their minds" about things.

Based on very little data, people and things become known for something. And the more someone comes in contact with something or hears about something, their mental "filing cabinet" swells with content. And to simplify all of this content, they tend to write on the invisible folder tab a brief overview of what it's known for or what we may want to remember it for. It's a thread of continuity that holds your "parts" together.

We're all known for something.

Do I need to remind you of this? Based on what others have written on the mental "file folder," you've been summed up. It could be true. It could be wildly wrong. It could be for something you don't want. Remember though that perception becomes their reality.

What I'm talking about here is that you *can* intentionally choose to be known for something and even change the label on the folder.

It's about being intentional.

How It Happens

Actors, politicians, and marketers are excellent at doing it. We see it playing out continuously. Yet, we somehow think it's too complicated to do for ourselves. But it's not.

Let's take a look at real-world examples:

Robert Downey, Jr. is an actor who started out strong with a brilliant career in TV and movies. Then, numerous drug-related arrests for cocaine, heroin, and marijuana had him in and out of drug rehab. Many had written him off. He became known for being a loser.

Then, the *Iron Man* franchise was introduced, and 2008 was a huge year for him. Many people knew he was a good actor but with a losing personal life. This changed with the half-billion dollars that was earned on the movie and a lot of positive publicity. Then, he became known for being a quirky, yet amazing actor. You may only remember him for being Tony Stark. He changed the label on our filing folders.

Brittany Spears was known as Disney's *Mickey Mouse Club* singer with an amazing voice. Soon, she tumbled into a life that was out of control, shaving her head and landing in a psychiatric ward.

But then, she made a comeback. Now, many know her for a fairly successful Vegas run with over 100 million albums sold. Another label changed.

Justin Bieber, Whitney Houston, and Lindsay Lohan: You probably know them for something as well.

Why It's Important

The benefits of being known for the right things are gigantic. You need to come to mind when someone needs a specific thing on a regular basis. And if a bunch of people are looking for that thing, it could be gold. It's called "top-of-mind awareness," being the first person or organization that comes to mind for something. It's your thread. I call that "being known for something."

You can be known for something based on three things:

- **What people know**
- **What people perceive about you**
- **What you tell people about you**

I was raised as a "regular" lower-middle-class kid. I wasn't extraordinary in school. I had an active imagination. In elementary and middle school, I was known for bending the truth when pressed, doing the bare minimum in the classroom, not being athletic, and being quiet (unless I was acting or singing). I idolized my brother, Brent, who was one year older and seemed to do everything I wished I could do. I also idolized my sister, Joy, who was a couple years older and could do no wrong in my eyes.

Before I entered ninth grade, our church decided to open a Christian school. Being this was the late '70s, the Christian school movement hadn't yet taken off in our part of North America. My mom had just graduated from college at age 40 (the first college degree ever in our family) and had her elementary education degree. She had started teaching in the church school, so my parents asked if I'd be interested in attending there. I didn't really like public school, so I decided that anything was better than being picked on for being a Christian in the non-Christian education environment.

I developed friends and started to enjoy school. We only had one teacher for all the high school students, so I learned to set goals and become self-motivated. Because of the smaller class size, I tried out some leadership skills. What I discovered was that no one really knew the awkward Mark MacDonald from my public school life, so I could "try" to be anyone I wanted to be with little risk of someone bringing me back to reality.

Except my mother… who I can still remember catching my eye in the school hallway and giving me that look of "is that Mark doing that?" I could never tell whether it was disappointment or concern. But from my drama background and from my abilities to twist the truth with a straight face, I realized I could create (or recreate) who I was by being confident with the idea and being consistent with it.

By the time I went to college, 1400 miles away and with no one to catch my eye to remind me who I was, I had subconsciously developed a process for success.

My parents dropped me off that first day on campus in South Carolina, and I remember entering my dorm room after my parents drove away. I realized I had two reactions. I could wallow in the fact that I knew no one, or I could once again use my newfound existence as a stage to prepare myself for what I wanted to be known for. I chose the latter.

I remember having a quiet time one morning at my desk in my room and praying that God would allow me to have a fresh start. I realized I could be anyone I wanted to be with God's help. No one was there to remind me of my past, and no one was going to stop me except for myself.

Know what you want to be known for, and create goals (or steps) that will push you along that specific path. Then, throughout the process, remind yourself and others around you who you are. This is marketing.

Some people view marketing as evil, an excuse to lie. Because I've been transparent about my propensity to bend truth, I should stop and tell you that bending truth is lying. And God also calls that a sin.

We're not supposed to lie. We should avoid it. And like the Old Testament story of Joseph and Potiphar's wife, when we come close to anything that tempts us, it's better for us to flee. Run as fast as you can from it. It's better to leave the area than to be tempted into acting on something that's wrong.

I've built stop-gap measures into my life to keep me from lying. I'm repulsed by lies. Good marketing is not lying.

So, what is *Christian* marketing? It's essentially changing your path, if needed, and emphasizing the right path that you're authentically on.

I realize that the discussion seems like this book is only about changing perception… but not exactly.

Sometimes, we can be known for something that isn't compelling. Boring. Not needed. These aren't bad perceptions, but my intention with this book is to show you how to have *great* relevance and influence in your community. To revitalize your church's reputation.

Relevance and influence are critical.

In my creative positions at the large agency, we were blessed to have significant influence with our greater geographic region even though our agency was actually located in a very small college town. Because I sang regularly at the "big church" in the heart of downtown, I became known as a singer in this small community. Because the funeral home was only a stone's throw from our creative offices, I often used my afternoon coffee breaks to run next door to sing at funerals. I became known as a funeral singer. So, I've been to more funerals than most people.

As I would sit through the final service of total strangers, I'd hear family members explaining the importance of the person laid out in the casket. I often listened intently so I could try to sing greater meaning into the songs that had been selected for me.

Sadly, many times, the story was merely that "he was born, had some friends, worked hard, fought a brilliant fight, and then died." How sad and hopeless.

Being a funeral singer taught me something: **I want to be known for more than that.**

I want to be remembered for something when I die. And more importantly, I want to be known for something throughout my life that points to Christ and for my life to benefit the world in which I live.

I want to be known for the right thing and to be consistent with it. Will you join me? You can do it, too.

And as you lead your church into revitalizing your reputation, you will have a huge impact on your community.

Discussion #5

Look around. What do friends and acquaintances know each of us for? Share with each other what you know them for and how that perception was established. (If you're alone, ask a good friend for the answer about you.)

What about our church? What does the community know us for? What about our congregation?

What solution(s) are we (and our church) needed for? Is there a correlation between what we're known for and the solutions we provide?

Are we truly content with what we're known for? If not, what would we like to be known for? Think about what our community needs.

Want additional information, downloads, and worksheets? Join us at www.beknownbook.com.

6

THE THREAD PRINCIPLE

When you have clear vision with consistent implementation, people will be drawn to you.

To be known for something, you must reinforce the idea continuously in the same manner to the same people.

I have found that most people like continuity, having things somewhat consistent each time we experience something or someone. We like going to a restaurant and having an amazing meal with just the right food, the right service, and the right environment. That's when we're quick to share it with a friend so he or she can experience it, too. There's nothing worse than bring-ing someone back with you and having a bad experience.

Inconsistency leads people into negative emotions or concerns that prevent them from talking about you positively.

In relationships, whether with a friend, spouse, or co-worker, we strive to find people who are consistent with their actions, mo-tives, and words. We want them to be somewhat predictable but not boring, of course. "Who they are" is that generalization label or thread that we assign to someone based on a level of consistency.

I have several friends who people describe as "creative." In fact, I've been described that way, too. Often, I'm amazed by what that ultimately means to most people. Often, it means random, impulsive, or plain crazy. It seems that anyone who does odd things and "out-of-the-box" crazy stuff will have people calling them creative or, worse, eccentric. Often, it seems to work for them, or so it seems, so they try to do even more random acts and say random things. But for anyone who has tried to continue this kind of relationship, it becomes confusing and tiring. We all want to expect some sort of normal that glues someone together in our minds. What most people think is attractive in creativity (randomness and quirkiness) actually pushes other people away.

Creatives need to push toward consistency and resist being too random.

When geologists dig into the earth's surface, they expect to find layers. If they're looking for gold (or another ore), they know they will discover a connected thread that will take them on a journey below the earth's crust... a golden thread, if you will. God has built into His creation threads of connectivity that allow us to see order. If we look for threads, we'll find them everywhere because God is the God of order.

And because we're made in His image, we tend to be attracted to and expect order in our lives.

God's Word has a thread, too.

God's Word, the Bible, also has a consistency of plot and theme from beginning to end.

Starting in the *Book of Genesis*, we see the creation of man and how God made it perfect. Then, man chose his own desires that were contrary to God's instruction. Sin, therefore, required a dire punishment: death (separation from God). So, God demonstrated how a specific offering would appease His wrath. The Bible continues with each book of the Old Testament describing and demonstrating that cycle... and, ultimately, our need for a perfect Offering.

Finally, the New Testament introduces us to Him, Jesus. Each book in the New Testament continues with this "new" order instructing us concerning how we should live within our relationship with Jesus and the Holy Spirit. The 66 books end with Jesus sitting on the throne, having His redeemed people gathered around Him in Heaven.

Many people read these books and see them as separate short stories, but when God breathed these books into existence, He created a unifying theme, the divine theme of Jesus.

You can flip open the pages of the Bible and start reading anywhere. And as soon as you know that the redemptive blood of Jesus has been drizzled over the foundation of each book, you can understand the fuller meaning and quickly tie the stories and doctrines to the ultimate theme of the Bible.

The Bible is known for the saving, redeeming power of the perfect God-given sacrifice, Jesus. He was crucified, and His blood atoned for our sins. That blood has been woven intentionally throughout scriptures as the unifying thread that bonds the Bible together, the Scarlet Thread.

Thread of Consistency

We need a thread of consistency in our lives to be known for something. But many think this approach would make us seem monotonous. Not true. Focusing on one thread doesn't have to be boring when it's done properly. The Bible has proven this. Just like a ball of yarn can look and feel totally different when made into a garment, a blanket, a wall hanging, etc., your message (thread) can and should look different depending on who's looking at it, using it, or enjoying it.

Almost every day after elementary school as a youngster, I had the habit of coming home and plopping myself down in our small basement family room in our family's bungalow. Like many in the 1970s, we always had one or two of those crocheted throws on our sofas. They had the loose, open holes that your fingers could easily go through. Some were scratchy while others had softer yarns that allowed them to feel warmer. My grandmother carefully made many of them for us. Because we were living in Canada and because our TV was in a small basement room, most of my memories of watching television included laying on the pull-out sofa and being wrapped in one of these coarse, hand-crafted throws. As most children do, I would subconsciously play with whatever was near.

One day after fiddling with a loose yarn end, I realized the strand had become longer. It seemed to have happened almost magically. I'd like to believe it was out of curiosity more than stupidity that I watched as this small end of yarn became longer and longer as I pulled on it. Without missing the plot of *Hogan's Heroes* that was emanating from our old, black-and-white TV cabinet, I continued to perform this wonderful magic trick. After what seemed like only a few moments, I realized that a quarter of the throw was now laying in a heap of polyester yarn in my lap.

That handmade throw (or should I say hand-*destroyed* throw) shows how one long yarn thread can be modified to create something that is more attractive and has a great purpose. The yarn becomes secondary to the way the yarn is used. So often do we forget about the yarn while enjoying its utility. Like the throw, the Bible can also be unraveled to demonstrate the Scarlet Thread of Jesus. Many pastors refer to this as "unpacking" the Scripture passage.

So what should the Christian's thread be?

In Philippians 2:5, the Bible says we are to be known for reflecting (mirroring) Jesus. This will cause people to know we are Christ-followers by our love. It's only through Jesus that we can have that selfless love. His Scarlet Thread should be crocheted throughout our lives so that every action in our workplaces, with our checkbooks, or among our families can be quickly tied back to the ultimate Scarlet Thread in our lives.

Our churches, which are collections of Christ-followers, need to be known for love, too. It's what many call our "witness." And I guess it's Satan that, like a child who pulls the wrong thread, wants to unravel the masterpiece that God's trying to complete in each of us.

Being known for something is ultimately about knowing what that thread is in our lives.

Knowing the Scarlet Thread in the Bible lets us unpack God's Word so much differently than would someone who doesn't understand it. We need to tell others continually about the blood of Christ. It's always there in Scripture, but it's up to us to point to it.

I guess the question is this: "Shouldn't we, as believers, all be known for Jesus then?"

Absolutely. So I guess you can put the book down and live your life as a direct connection to the Scarlet Thread. Seriously, I would be happy with that. And, more importantly, God would be, too!

But I believe we need to be known for something else as well that attracts our communities so they'll start to follow our thread and realize that it's attached to Jesus. If other believers are doing what they should be (and they're known for being redeemed by Jesus), the world will see the ultimate connection to Christ who is the reason we're trying to gain their attention.

The Four Thread Principles

1: There's one continuous thread.

Yes, the Scarlet Thread is the ultimate "end" to your strand, but you need one continuous similarity that leads to it, helping you to become known for something through your consistency.

2. The thread is interesting and meets a prominent need.

The main idea of your thread is something that is ultimately needed as a solution or a path to a goal. If it's not a solution or a path, it's often forgotten.

3: The thread can look like many things.

Like the books of the Bible that were penned by different authors and contain different themes, wildly different plots, and even different languages, the thread is still there. Sometimes, it's a stretch, but its DNA is infused within. The thread can be "knit" differently so it looks differently and eliminates boredom as it is consistently promoted. This is especially true when the thread is used with various ministries in a church.

4. Your thread ultimately is connected to the Scarlet Thread.

If you're a Christian, a Christian church, or an organization that demonstrates Christian values, you're connected to the Scarlet Thread of the Bible. Jesus is the beginning, the middle, and the end.

Being known for something is all about your thread. You need to discover it so it can unify your ministries, activities, and motives, enabling your community to understand you better and need you more.

Discussion #6

Is there any consistent thread about who we currently are? Are there regular themes that establish a thread? Or have there been too many changes within our communications that no one would ever be able to identify it?

If we do have a thread, how does it attach to the Scarlet Thread? Is it fairly easy to make the turn toward talking about Jesus from your thread? In other words, if someone knows us for a solution, how can we link that to the gospel story? The "closer" that link is, the easier it will be to be known for Jesus.

Discuss the steps between our solution thread and Jesus. Ever played the "Six Degrees of Kevin Bacon" game where someone can link almost any actor to Kevin Bacon in six steps? How many steps are we away from Jesus?

Want additional information, downloads, and worksheets? Join us at www.beknownbook.com.

7
ESTABLISHING A CHURCH THREAD

I've been so blessed to live in the United States since 2000. For almost all of it, I've run a church branding agency.

I've come from a line of entrepreneurs. My grandfather Mac-Donald (actually "McDonald," but that's a long story) ran a successful vegetable and fruit farm. After my dad retired from a long career in telephony, he and my mom repaired bicycles and had one of the largest showrooms of new and used bicycles and parts in our community.

When you run a business, the lines become blurred between the company and yourself. I have found myself preferring "we" rather than "me" because it's rarely me single-handedly doing anything. Rarely does any one person "control" everyone in their group. You can be known for something on an individual level, but how do you get everyone in the group to be known for the same thing?

This, too, is critical when we talk about the local church. There's a complexity of pastors, leaders, volunteers, and the congregation coupled with the layers of various ministries.

That's why the we focus on branding. It's simply the wrapper that an entire group is known for. It allows individuals flexibility to operate under your brand's story.

Here are four things you must understand in order to create an umbrella brand that will be known for something:

1: Know who will decide.

You may call yourself "in charge," and others may even say you're in charge. It doesn't take me very long in an initial church meeting to realize that the senior pastor or manager is not really in control of everything. Usually, it's never truly one person. Think about who you rely on to make decisions. Who do you ask for their opinions to "help formulate" yours? You'll need to create a small group (less than 6-8 people) that will walk with you through this process on behalf of your church. These should be people who are committed to the organization and aren't on their way out, and they should have some level of authority in the church.

2: Get as much input as possible.

Everyone on this leadership team must feel free to discuss everything about your organization. Sometimes, I enter this meeting and realize everyone represented ultimately is a "yes" person for the senior leader. If everyone is simply going to agree with one person, there's very little value in having them on the team. Everyone must have a voice, an honest opinion, and the passion to be heard. It's critical to the process. You don't want to hear, "I was going to tell you that earlier, but now that we're nearing the approval stage, I'd better."

3: Obtain buy-in.

Once you've worked through this process with everyone on the team, they must all decide to follow the thread. Everyone in the organization must understand and feel the importance of the thread. People can disagree behind closed doors but must be unified when the doors are open. Rogue leaders drive wedges in relationships and bore holes in the bottom of the boat. Not only will mutiny break out, but the boat will sink around the fighting. Ministry silos, where individual ministries seek to have importance outside of the overall church thread, need to be torn down.

4: Evaluate regularly.

Because several leadership layers are often involved who represent the larger group, it's critical to have intentional meetings to discuss successes and failures. This is your opportunity for course correction. And these changes must be decided on by the entire group yet again. No rogue explorers!

As you will see in the next section, the process can work for your church or organization. Except, it will require intentionality, time, commitment, and motivation to unite the larger group. Just remember that this process doesn't describe *you*; it describes the thread you all are committing to be represented by. Granted, the church wrapper can often become your personal mantra, causing the line between you and your church to become blurred. This is not a problem except when course corrections from the team disagree with you personally. And then, you need to resolve that disagreement, or it could mean leaving the group.

Discussion #7

Who would be on a team of people to make the final decision for our church? How will we decide that?

Are there any leaders listed above who are antagonistic toward the leadership? It's often better to get their differing point of view before you establish the thread than after when you ask them to adopt it.

How will we ensure everyone adopts the thread?

How will we evaluate our thread regularly?

Want additional information, downloads, and worksheets? Join us at www.beknownbook.com.

Part 3

BE WORTH KNOWING

8

KNOW YOUR TWO COMMUNITIES

*Strategy starts with the fundamental choice of
which customers to pursue.*

—DAVID BURKUS, ASSISTANT PROFESSOR OF MANAGEMENT AT
ORAL ROBERTS UNIVERSITY

Ready to get started? Really want to be known for something? I
hope I hear a resounding "yes!" It'll take self-awareness, foundational research, the proper tools, creativity, and consistency. But
it'll pay off. Being known for the right things will endear you to
your community and allow you to help it turn to Christ. In general, the Church has lost its connection to the communities where
the buildings and people are located. This process reconnects
your ministries to its core community. Whether you're finding
yourself in a slump or your ministry is in full decline, this strategy
will realign you and, if done properly, will cause revitalization
and start growth as you're being empowered by the Holy Spirit
and prayer.

To get started, we're going to examine three simple things:

- Your two communities (or audiences)
- Your product or service
- Your benefit or relevance

No matter how many times I meet with a group, most problems rise and fall on not knowing the intended audience. In order to have relevance or to influence someone, you have to understand that "someone." If something is failing in your church, go back to this critical foundation. Know your audience!

Your Primary Audience: The Community Where You're Located

Wouldn't it be great if you could step on the world's stage and instantly be known for something? Many of us call this fame or instant success. But it's so rare that anyone does this. The path to the top is often becoming known for something at many plateaus.

I heard Jay Leno discussing his more than 20 years as host of *The Tonight Show* on NBC (Jan 30, 2014, *The Ellen Show*). He explained that the difference between his standup comedy career and his TV host career was in the different way in which jokes are told across these two formats. He explained that, when he tells a joke on the standup circuit, he'll tell it, watch for reactions, and over several subsequent tellings, the joke would get better each time. Jay lamented that, on his late-night TV show, he only had one chance to tell the joke, which is why it could so easily fall flat. He would never be quite sure of whether a joke would be successful until the audience gave feedback... on live television! Yikes!

Success arrives from being prepared through much practice for the moment when an opportunity arises. I'm glad I wasn't given an opportunity to stand on a national stage initially until I had many smaller stages on which to practice. Many big failures happen because people haven't been given smaller opportunities that would have refined them through smaller failures. That's how we get better. Don't try to capture a large audience until you've captivated a small audience's attention first.

Tackling a smaller audience is also wise because it's costly to reach a large audience. We've had clients share with us that they have a product that the entire United States needs. Yes, for a fortune, we could reach every American. It can be done. But it's better to reach success and the cashflow that comes with it by targeting a smaller, defined audience first and then using that tested momentum to reach beyond.

My first branding and advertising agency was called Pin-Point Creative (*Be Known For Something* was developed from PinPoint's positioning). Naming the agency was excruciating and required brainstorming with another talented branding guru. Pinpointing an audience is critical for all marketing communication. That's why we agreed to the name after many rounds of discussion. And the smaller the audience that can be pinpointed, the easier it is to influence that audience.

For your church on a corporate level, I'd recommend identifying your smaller reach audience. This is the reasonable, local area that your church can reach for Christ. Here are the steps to identifying that area:

1. Plot on a map where your current congregational families live.
2. Start looking for trends and clusters.
3. Identify a radius from your church where most live (ignore outliers as anomalies) or create a polygon shape that runs along major highways or geographic divides (e.g. rivers, mountain ranges, interstates, large subdivisions, or highways).

This is your church's reach area.

On a personal level as a ministry leader, I would suggest identifying your immediate audience before attempting to influence a larger community. These people already know you quite well and understand what you have to offer them. You live around them, interact with them, and can communicate to them without too much effort. Thanks to social media, we all have this small audience within our arms' length. But they also represent the people with whom you work, play sports, and run into around the community.

This is your smaller, personal reach area, which is a subset of the church's overall reach area.

You need to identify the smallest group that is your sphere of influence and then, in concentric circles, identify the next larger group and the next larger group beyond that. In Acts 1:8, Jesus tells His disciples to go to Jerusalem (the inner circle), Judea and Samaria (the next larger region), and the uttermost parts of the world (your ultimate goal). It's easier to start in your smallest area and move outward, building on your successes.

Michael Hyatt's book, *Platform*, is a fascinating read about how to develop your audience if you want to jump into this subject deeper.

Why is understanding your audience so critical?

It allows you to look at similarities within your group. "Birds of a feather" really do tend to flock together. If there's a group, there's almost always a good reason they're together. If you're reaching some people in an area, there are, most likely, others in that area who need what you're offering, too.

Demographics is the science of identifying the similarities of the people who have flocked together. It's understanding the ages, gender, occupations, and other measurable information about groups. This is rarely subjective as it's usually objective polls or censuses that provide the information.

Psychographics are a bit harder to determine. It's taking the demographics and assigning what we know about those definitive groups: how they feel, their likes and dislikes, and most importantly, fairly accurately identifying what their pains, concerns, needs, wants, and goals are.

Understand the demographic and psychographic similarities in your reach areas so you can know why a group of people have clustered together. We must understand their needs because those needs are what motivate people to an action or decision like choosing your ministries, attending a service, or listening to you.

Abraham Maslow produced a secular research paper in 1943, "A Theory of Human Motivation," in which he discussed human needs. He proposed that there are five basic needs that are prioritized in this order (most important first): physiological, safety & security, love & belonging, self-esteem, and self-actualization. Ultimately, if someone has a physiological need, it needs to be solved or quenched in order to care about safety. And so on.

SELF ACTUALIZATION
SELF ESTEEM
LOVE & BELONGING
SAFETY & SECURITY
PHYSIOLOGICAL NEEDS

‑ ‑ ‑ ‑ ‑ ‑

MASLOW'S HIERARCHY OF NEEDS

SELF-FULFILLMENT < PSYCHOLOGICAL < BASIC

Understanding felt needs of the people in your specific community can help you to understand what they want. If someone is really thirsty, being known for quenching thirst would be a great thing. This is the reconnection a church needs with its community!

Jesus did an amazing job of identifying needs and dealing with a basic root need before dealing with another need farther up the hierarchy.

In John 4, Jesus demonstrated these skills. We have so much to learn from Him, which is a total understatement! Here are three lessons from that Bible story that we need to heed...

Jesus went to where He knew there would be a person in need.

Scripture said that, on His long journey, He stopped to rest at Jacob's Well in Sychar, a great place to stop if you want to have an identifiable need! Do you know where "thirsty" people are in your reach community? Are you visiting that location regularly, waiting for a needy person to stop by? We need to be available in the right places. Jesus sometimes got away from His group of disciples, which may be an indication that more ministry can be done outside of our church gatherings. We must stop waiting for the community to come to us. Let's go to them.

Jesus supplied a temporal solution in order to deliver an eternal message.

Jesus, the unexpected communicator, got the woman's attention first by engaging with the topic of water (the basic solution to her temporal need). Then, the subject of *water* transitioned into a discussion about *living water*. Jesus said, "But whoever drinks of the water that I will give... will never be thirsty again." That's making the turn to the eternal!

What are you able to provide to your needy community so that you can share Christ's love? A foundational temporal need will surely engage them. Then, they'll eventually listen to spiritual solutions as you make "the turn."

Jesus made the turn.

Churches often are doing a major disservice to their communities as they're providing what's needed temporally without making the ultimate connection to the prevailing spiritual problem. All of our problems are caused by sin, and only One can solve our sin issue. Jesus is the eternal solution to people's needs, so we must make the turn to talk about Him, or we're merely doing great humanitarian projects.

I travel a lot to help churches across the U.S., so I tell my Bible class to pray for the unsuspecting person who'll sit next to me on flights. These individuals will probably talk about things they never thought they would on a flight. That's why I ask my class to pray that they'll be open to the discussion and that I'll be able to make the leap from the temporal conversation into a deeper conversation.

May our churches pinpoint their reach communities, identify the temporal needs that are top of mind, engage with them by providing a solution, and then make the leap to the spiritual. That's good church communications.

It's fairly easy for me to be friendly and talk with someone to identify what their needs are, especially if I can figure out their age or stage of life. It's the ability to make the turn to talking about the spiritual that requires the intervention of the Holy Spirit and my willingness.

I've had the privilege of sharing dozens of stories with my class where I've had the opportunity to share my faith, pray with people, and even cry with those who are hurting. These things would never have happened unless I had taken the leap.

Fundamentally, that's being willing to strategize where to wait, what to share, and how to connect them to Jesus. That can be done online, in person, or in print. It just needs to be anticipated beforehand so we can be prepared.

Pastors and ministry leaders, it's this preparation that this book is all about. It's about being known for something corporately that engages with a community so that every person in your congregation knows how to make the turn to a conversation about Christ.

It all starts with reconnecting with your community and their needs. Where can you get the demographic information?

There are many sources. Research can be found online, from the government, and from demographic companies like Percept Group who sell ministry-based data for reach areas. They compile secular demographic data as well as psychographic ministry data such as music preference and architectural style preference for places of worship plus many other details that will help you to visualize and understand your community.

Try to discover what the trends are for your community. Demographic projections are priceless as we must understand the changes and prepare for them. Many demographic studies will provide three or five-year projections.

Your Secondary Audience: Your Congregation

Once you have researched your external reach area, you need to compare it to who you are currently in your church, your internal community... your congregation.

I debated discussing this section first but decided that most churches focus almost entirely inwardly. The navel gazing that we call vision or mission-planning usually drives us into ourselves, who we are, and why we exist. After countless meetings and months of discussion, a church decides why they are who they are, why their programs are good, and where the congregation should head in the future, according to its leadership and the Bible.

Often, the church lands on a long, pithy paragraph that they proudly debate, approve, and place on their website and in their foyer. The church leadership (may) remember it, but rarely does anyone in the pews have the mental capacity to remember its complexity.

To know your vision and mission is good, except that no one in the community will be drawn to a church vision or mission. Only other church people in the community will be attracted to the spiritual nuance of it. The purpose of this book is to help you to be known for something that will expand the Kingdom and reach deeply into the lost community. I want you to be light in the darkness that profoundly needs it. Therefore, I believe the church needs to examine the "potential audience" in the community primarily and decide what they need to be known for so that the community will be attracted to them. The local church should spring from the community and represent who the community is. Therefore, it's essential for us to understand our external community and then to understand who you are internally to make sure you balance that understanding with the external information.

Our communities are growing while our congregations are shrinking. Let's see the potential around us while, secondarily, making sure we understand our congregations and meet their needs. Let's create congregations that look and grow like our communities, churches that offer solutions to the needs of our communities.

Your church originally assembled for many reasons. If your church is growing, the reasons will be quite evident. But if you're not growing, your internal audience probably has lost sight of the benefit of attending, and your community isn't understanding any benefit either, or they're simply not aware of it.

You need to understand your congregation and who attends your church. Determining internal demographics is difficult because you're so close to the group. Don't be tempted to rely on your intuition. Research the actual numbers, or survey your people to get them.

Demographics You Need to Know

Someone in your church should have these numbers: what the average age is, what demographic groups are represented and what percentages they make up, and whether you have more females than males. Do you know their occupations? Are there similarities? Differences? Is there a shift happening? A simple

Survey Monkey survey (or something similar) can capture this information if you don't have it.

Compare the internal data with the external audience information.

Is your current audience similar? Different? How will that affect your approach going forward? How much change will you accomplish? Does your brand actually represent what it should?

Discover the pain, need, and goal similarities.

What does your external community need that is similar to your congregation? Is there a goal that unites the two audiences? How prevalent is it internally? Externally? Will it be ongoing, or is it diminishing? How is it being satisfied now? Is it only you in your area who is providing a solution? Who else is? Be careful, Church... Don't be quick to answer this with another church's name. On average, in America, the majority of people aren't having their spiritual needs satisfied by a church. Consider secular solutions that are satisfying the needs in your community. You need to be aware of these.

The information you've compiled, compared, and understood about your internal and external communities will allow you to become known for something that's needed, helping you to provide a solution to prominent concerns or a path to an important goal.

Review

Start with your smaller, targeted community who needs you, discover their similarities while paying close attention to their needs and goals, and consider how they're satisfying that need currently... whether through you or some other way.

Communication Personas

Research the demographics of your reach area, and create personas of your primary and secondary audiences. A communication persona is a fictitious person you create who represents an actual group that you're uniquely qualified to engage. This will allow you to direct and clarify your messages as you focus your communications on who really matters, your core audience.

Here's how you can create communication personas:

1: Identify your groups.

Look at your internal community, and identify the ones who are fully engaged and interested in your ministry programs. Do they line up with a large enough group in your community? Ensure they connect, or you're setting up a ministry for a community who won't sustain your ministry. Questions to ask during this process:

- Imagine that your church disappeared. Who would miss you the most?
- When you're preaching or communicating to "most" of your congregation, who would that be? Who would be the close runner up? If necessary, decide on a tertiary audience.

Be careful not to have too many groups because this will complicate your communication process as you'll be trying to reach everyone rather than growing larger groups. Everyone will not be represented among your congregation or community, and that's fine. You only need a large portion.

Now, open a document, and start creating a description about them. Decide the average age of each group, whether they're skewed male or female, and whether there are other distinguishing characteristics.

2: Name them.

Come up with a name that you'll remember. We like to use a fictitious person's first name and a descriptor for the last name (e.g. Sarah Senior, Mathew Millennial, Hannah Homemaker, etc.). Later, we often refer to them by their first names as if we're friends because we get to know them that well! It's easier and less political to refer to your fictitious personas rather than real people or groups in your church.

3: Tell a story about them.

Now, the fun part. In a short paragraph, write a short story that reminds you who they are, what they do, and the story of their lives. Be descriptive enough that anyone in the group would identify with the generalizations if they read them. Then, create a list of needs, pains, and concerns that most of them would have. Complete your description with a list of goals that most would have for their lives.

4: Picture them.

Conduct an online search for people in that group, and choose a picture that represents the communication persona (e.g. Millennial male Hispanic, middle-aged business woman, etc.). All personas are for internal use only, so don't worry about the copyright of the image. (You can also narrow your search in Google Advanced Image search to shareable images to get pictures without copyrights.) Simply choose someone who looks like they're representative of your persona group. Grab his or her picture, and add it next to his or her name. Complete this process for each of the persona groups.

5: Talk to them.

Keep this persona sheet nearby when deciding what you need to be known for in your community. And while you're writing communication materials, talk directly to a persona with whom you're trying to engage. Want to get their attention? Name one of their concerns or goals, and suggest how your ministry programs are a solution to the concern or a path to the goal.

Caution

As a church, let's pause to remind you that ministries must represent all of a community (not just your personas). God loves your congregation and your community... everyone. He's called you to love them as He loves, and He's called the (universal) Church to reach *all* for Him... to share the gospel of Jesus Christ with everyone.

So why have personas? You can't reach everyone effectively. That's why local churches were planted, starting with Apostle Paul and continuing to this day. There are limitations of every church for reaching everyone. That's why there are so many local churches and why each church has a specific area and set of personas that they reach exceptionally well. All marketing principles rely on this. The smaller the segmented community, the easier it is to reach more of it.

It's easier to understand when we consider that, realistically, someone won't drive more than 20 miles to your church. It used to be that people wouldn't cross a natural divide (e.g. a river, a key highway, or a wooded area), but with the advent of mega-churches and a better sense of travel to get what we want (e.g. better highways, choices, better vehicles, etc.), people will travel much farther. Ultimately, we understand there's a limit. So we rely on another local church to reach them closer to their location.

Maybe you haven't considered though that there may be a psychological divide that keeps people from attending your church. It may be based on age, need, or… gulp… styles of worship. When this happens, you have to decide what you'll do. Should you create multiple church services for various prominent groups? Should you allow another local church to provide for that audience? Sadly, we can't reach everyone.

When it comes to personas, I'm not sure a local church should limit themselves entirely to specific groups though. This sounds like a contradiction, but it's something I wrestle with, and I'm not fully satisfied with how I balance secular marketing with church marketing. I do know that God loves everyone and that His gospel is for everyone. We do need to be sensitive to how groups of people respond to our styles and brands. Prayerfully analyze who is currently in your group, and try not to narrow excessively who they are. Always err on the side of being more inclusive.

But as discussed at the beginning of this chapter, it's true that birds of a feather flock together, so it'll be rare that you'll be able to attract someone outside of your communication personas for a long-term relationship. But God works miracles outside of what makes sense. There's a tension here that we all need to feel.

The Gospel Is for Everyone

Remain mindful that the gospel message is for everyone. God can use your ministries to deliver that message to anyone, but more likely, He will primarily use you to minister to people who are similar to your congregation. Engage with your community and all who live there, but understand that some may not feel comfortable inside your church. (They're probably not your main personas.) You can either set up a satellite church for these people, according to their demographic/psychographic personas, or you can refer them to another church who matches them better. Be careful not to demand that they change their cultures as you're capturing their hearts for Jesus. For the things in their lives that need to be changed, the Holy Spirit will work on them... hopefully, with your guidance.

Mystery Visits

I'm amazed by how many churches don't have a concept of what they're known for. I can't emphasize enough that you shouldn't trust your instincts. Our opinions of familiar things are usually skewed. It's the "can't-see-the-forest-for-the-trees" issue. We're too close to the situation to look at it in a balanced way.

We know people who truly think they're helpful while most people know they only cause stress when they're around. We all know the person who wants to be part of everything but doesn't ever add anything worthwhile. Our perceptions of ourselves are skewed and often wrong. Therefore, it's very difficult to view ourselves as others do.

Be Known For Something started a mystery visitor program a few years ago. One of our consultants will attend your church for the first time and provide an "outsider's" report. Sure, we do this as knowledgeable outsiders, but you can get anyone to do it for you. Here are five ways you can ensure that you get the proper feedback from a mystery visitor.

1: Use someone not connected with your church.

The mystery visitor needs to know the principles of marketing, branding, and being known for something. However, the person should not be connected with your church. There are companies who offer this service, but you can find someone from a nearby community to help you.

Caution: Do not use your church leadership. Do not use anyone who is politically connected to your leadership or congregation.

Though, use someone who understands church, your organization, and "who you want to be." Use a highly observant person who wants the best for your organization and can accurately state his or her opinion in a positive light.

2: Use someone who understands demographics.

With the knowledge of your community's demographics, the mystery visitor must "become" the persona (or personas) that you're trying to influence. For example, if your potential audience is predominantly a Millennial group, the person doing the mystery visit must "feel" like a 20-something. 1 Corinthians 9 says that Paul wanted to become all things to all people so that he might save some. You need to become a character actor of that persona so you can recognize issues and solutions. This isn't deception; it's an internal awareness that you must gain through the mystery visit. The ultimate goal is to lead people into the saving knowledge of Jesus Christ.

3: Make it a "cold" visit.

The church shouldn't be aware of when it will happen, and neither should the leadership. Be sure you don't conduct unusual preparation, or it won't be an accurate sample of your regular church services.

4: Involve the website and a maps application.

The mystery visitor must act like a legitimate visitor to the area. To do this accurately, they should scan the church website to find out what a visitor would seek before attending (e.g. service times, directions, what to wear, what to expect, etc.) and rely on that information. Then, on the way to church, the mystery visitor should ask Siri, use GPS, or rely on the directions from the website to discover where the church is located.

On one mystery visit I did for a church, I followed these steps. I had no idea how large the church would be from my discussion with the church leadership. I didn't know what to wear or where to find the church. I had flown to the community the night before without knowing *anything* about the church. From my hotel room, I looked at their website, found the service times, and made plans to attend the next morning. I asked Siri to find directions to the church and used that to plan on arriving 10 minutes before the service.

We do this regularly for large, medium-sized, and small churches. I never really know what to expect.

I followed Siri's directions that led me to the church entrance. I pulled into the parking lot and grew quite concerned that I was the fifth car in the lot, and it was 10 minutes before the service! I started wondering if my mystery visit would end up being only an observation of the pianist's family, the pastor's family, and a deacon's family.

I took a deep breath and proceeded. I looked around and didn't know where the main entrance was, and there was no one to ask. No signage. No indication on the two buildings that I could see. I decided that I must have parked on the back side of the building, so I ventured down the sidewalk between the buildings. As I got to the other side, I discovered I was in the middle of a large campus and had no idea where to go. I couldn't imagine being on such a large campus with so few people. I wondered if the website was wrong about the service times or if everyone had been spooked by the dusting of snow that had fallen the night before. It was confusing for me, yet I do this all the time!

Imagine what a first-time visitor would have been feeling and thinking. *I wonder what other church I should try.* I've seriously seen people drive in and out of a church parking lot without getting out. Perhaps it wasn't what they were expecting, they didn't feel welcome, or there was limited parking. It's sad.

Finally, I walked into a large building and saw two people (ushers getting ready for the service). I tried to look like a typical visitor who was unsure of where to go. They walked by me, discussing a sports game that had happened the night before.

I approached them and asked where the service was. They directed me to an adjacent building: "go outside and to the left." I proceeded outdoors to the correct building and, with relief, realized that the main parking lot (that was almost full) was on the other side of the campus, and I was entering a large worship center with a congregation eager to worship. What happened? Siri (Apple Maps) had directed me to the wrong entrance of this very large church. Something so simple could've kept me from their wonderful service.

5: Require a full, organized report.

Everyone who is part of your leadership team (and especially those responsible for guest hospitality) need to be part of a debriefing. Without excuses or justifications, listen, take notes about what was discovered, and ask how to correct the issues. This must be an honest discussion rather than becoming vindictive. Ask plenty of questions! It's your time to find out what you're known for when people arrive for the first time.

Based on mystery visits I've done personally, most congregations have become used to a process or a system but don't encounter first-time visitors regularly, so they've become lax. A mystery visit is a great wakeup call for your team as they get to hear from a person not connected to your church. A mystery visitor can unearth truths that you can't discover any other way.

Focus groups help you listen.

An additional approach to discover your current audience is to hire a facilitator to conduct focus groups. Focus groups are small groups of potential or current personas who are asked to meet and have a discussion. The facilitator needs to follow similar requirements for the mystery visitor except that it will be more obvious that the church is pursuing the information. This is a great way to understand your personas and understand their demographics.

Focus groups are about starting the conversation and listening. Let the groups set the agenda rather than controlling the conversation too much. You need them to have a voice, so listen well.

Ultimately, you need to know, understand, and anticipate what your internal and external community personas are feeling currently so that you can decide if something you're doing is building a wall between them and your ministry products. Eliminate all the barriers that would allow you to engage your two communities!

Discussion #8

Who are our two audiences? Who do we know better? Who do we need to know better?

Does our congregation represent our community in demographics and psychographics? Do you truly know? How can you find the data to confirm your speculation?

Are the needs of your congregation similar to the needs of your community?

Describe the gaps between our two audiences. Do the gaps need to be removed or reduced? How?

Name our primary and secondary communication personas (based on our community and hopefully our congregation). Take the time to tell their story, concentrating on their needs and goals. Write their descriptions down so we can determine if we're helping them with each ministry.

Who is a good person to do a mystery visit for us?

Have we talked regularly to our persona groups? Do we need to set up some focus groups?

How do we balance having personas and reaching everyone with the Gospel?

Want additional information, downloads, and worksheets? Join us at www.beknownbook.com.

9
KNOW YOUR PRODUCT

Does your church have something to offer to your community? That's your *product*; it can also be called a *service*.

When I was a young kid, I was out playing on a warm afternoon in our neighborhood. There were several other kids around our house, and we were hot and sweaty. I ran inside to get a drink of Kool-Aid because my mother had just finished making an ice-cold pitcher.

She asked if any of my friends wanted some. I realized they would because we were all hot, and it was thirst quenching! I took the pitcher out with lots of glasses. As we gulped down the sugary goodness, we started talking about how others in our area would love to enjoy some, too. My entrepreneurial blood started to pulse, and the proverbial neighborhood Kool-Aid stand was assembled for one of my first businesses.

I realized there was an audience who needed something, and if I could supply a reasonable solution for more money than it took to make it, I would help others and be rewarded for it.

Fast forward several years. A good friend of mine, who was an amazing children's pastor, and I were driving between our city and the next one over. It was a rural area, and the houses were back away from the busy highway and sat between large, forested areas. Kevin was driving, and we almost went through the windshield when he screeched to a halt in front of a driveway.

"What are you doing?" I asked.

Down the long, rural driveway, quite some distance from the road, was a rickety table and three very excited kids selling Orange Tang.

As we drove slowly down the driveway, Kevin explained that he wouldn't ever drive past a group of kids with a drink stand without using the opportunity to talk with the kids and reward their pursuits. He certainly understands community ministry.

Granted, after seeing the dirty pitcher and the muddy hands that served it, I doubted how smart it was to stop. Kevin, not missing a beat and obviously having done it many times before, asked for his Tang in a to-go cup. We paid for our drinks, talked to the kids about their church and whether they liked it, and truly made a nice connection with them. We got into the car and sheepishly disposed of the scary drinks as we continued down the road.

A drink stand can teach a lot about marketing and engaging people. It requires an available audience who likes what's being served enough to have it quench their thirst. Location is also important, but much thought must go into the product that is being sold! For your church, your product or service is vitally important to the success of your congregation. Ultimately, it's the foundation of what you'll be known for.

For most churches, the ministry programs have been multiplying as we hope to supply our congregations with just the right products. I wish that the amount of programs correlated to increasing membership, but it usually doesn't.

Churches today have a hard time stopping programs once they've been started. When they start, there seems to be a need or a desire for the program. It seems like a great idea or something that's popular at the time. Then, participation dwindles over time, yet the failing program continues to be listed on the church calendar.

People attend where they get a benefit.

If numbers are in decline, you must understand what's causing the decline. Utilizing church resources to push ministries that aren't working is not good stewardship.

Take a long look at your programs and decide which ones you should keep and which should be stopped. The surprising truth? Many larger churches have a very simple suite of programs. To read more about this, I'd recommend *Simple Church: Returning to God's Process for Making Disciples* by Thom S. Rainer and Eric Geiger.

Required Characteristics for a Church Program

It must meet needs.

In the commercial world, many products are created every day. The ones people think are worthy of greatness are submitted for patents. According to the U.S. Patent and Trademark Office (USPTO), an average of a quarter million patent applications have been submitted each year over the last decade.[1] That's almost 700 per day! Obviously, not all of them are successful although some go on to TV stardom through infomercials.

Let's take a look at what makes a great infomercial. Think about products like the Perfect Bacon Bowl, Choptastic, Hurricane Spin Mop, Tummy Tuck, Furniture Fix, Chillow, and more. When you watch a successful infomercial, they seem to put a lot of information into the 30-, 60-, or 120-second commercial. The advertiser's goal is to convince you that the product will solve a nagging problem. With over-dramatization, the advertiser tries to illustrate a problem you may have. For example, the advertiser may inform you about how terrible it is that you can't use your hands to fry eggs when they're hidden under a blanket and will then demonstrate how happy you'll be when their new product solves this problem for you. The more they convince you of the need in your life, the more inclined you'll be to pick up the phone to order it for $19.99.

This should be a communication formula for the church because we all have needs. Your successful church product should be associated with a particular need that your congregation is aware of. If not, be sure to emphasize the problem in order to attract their attention to the solution your program provides.

Do you know the solutions you're offering for each of your programs?

It must be unique.

Even if your church understands needs and delivers solutions, it still may not attract people. Scarcity of a particular solution makes it more valuable. In order to understand the value of your product, you must research how many others are supplying the solution. If it's everywhere, people will lower the value of it. If your church simply has everything that most other churches have, the potential audience in your community sees you as being just like all the other churches. You're a church. And most of them don't want "church."

To be known generically as a "church" becomes a barrier to them attending. Instead, we need to become known for providing a unique solution that may even surprise them, something that every other church doesn't communicate. Can you even imagine what that might be?

Let's suppose your demographic study of your reach area shows that your community is struggling with divorce and separation. Even in that tumultuous time, most people going through it don't turn to the church to help. Instead, they seek secular counselors and lawyers. To meet this particular need among your audience, your church could become known for cultivating healthy marriages. Someone who's struggling with his or her marriage may not come to your church service but may engage with your church to receive tips for saving his or her marriage. If you discover how others are marketing to the pre-divorce crowd, you can uniquely position your church because your church has a unique perspective on marriage.

People are willing to participate in a truly unique program. They may even attend a church because of it.

What if your programs aren't that unique? Secular marketing develops new categories to create scarcity. Instead of just another toothbrush, they develop a complete oral-hygiene device or maybe a customizable, 3-D printed, faster, "whole mouth" cleaner. If you're perceived as a non-unique commodity, try creating a new category so you can offer something that is scarce. A megachurch does this by being one of the largest churches in the area.

Creating scarcity will require creativity, but you should communicate your differences and not your similarities in ministry.

It must be available.

In your efforts to offer a solution that is scarce, don't become so scarce that you're not easily accessible. Otherwise, people may turn to another solution... even one that is less beneficial. How many times have you caught yourself running to a drugstore wanting something to solve a specific problem and then, after discovering it's not available, opting for a lesser cure?

Being in the right place at the right time for the right purpose is essential for your church.

For this reason, satellite church locations and adding service times are popular. If your programs are meeting needs, and you discover that you can provide your unique solution in a different area, a video venue may be a good option for your church.

It must be memorable.

If people can't remember your product, you're doomed. Proper naming is required to be memorable. A program's name can be a bit clever so as to stick in people's minds or really obvious so people can understand and remember it. But if it's not highly memorable, be creative with your communications to make it remembered.

Be careful, though, not to be *too* creative in the pursuit of being memorable.

Any name that needs an explanation is usually not a good option because people won't pursue the explanation and it would require a large promotional budget to educate your audience. Make the name and concept memorable in another way, something that will "stick" in the minds of your community's members. Many good solutions die because they are easily forgotten. To read more about being sticky in marketing, I'd suggest *Sticky Church* by Larry Osborne.

It must be consistent.

Your product must be delivered in a consistent manner; otherwise, people will stop using it.

We have a restaurant near our home that someone told me has great food and a "wonderful environment." I went with my wife and was delighted about this newfound treasure. I was even willing to pay their higher prices to enjoy the ambience. A client was coming through town, so I took him to this restaurant. You guessed it… The service wasn't very good that time, and the food was substandard. I tried it two or three more times, and it was hit-or-miss. I'm not tempted to eat there now because of the inconsistency.

Are your church services sometimes good and sometimes bad? Or are you known for how good they are? Is the solution you provide occasionally not delivered? Inconsistency will kill a product faster than any other issue. Create a process-oriented environment to ensure consistency!

The Power of New

Marketers also realize that, when you're promoting a product, there's a natural life cycle. It's the life cycle bell curve we talked about previously. A great new product usually gains momentum because the criteria listed above are communicated properly. Growth ensues. Then, a combination of market saturation (when most of the people in your area who needed your solution have discovered it), additional competition (when others realize they can provide a similar solution to your audience), and product boredom (when people start looking for other answers) occurs, there's a leveling of the product growth. This "top" of the bell curve shows up in offerings, attendance, and demand for a church.

Before this flattening occurs, it's time to do something "new."

If no innovation occurs, almost always, a precipitous decline on the other side of the bell curve plays out. Once decline starts, it has been my experience that the drop picks up momentum like a roller coaster tumbling down a steep slope.

If your church is in decline, it will be much harder for you to reinvent yourself and turn everything around. It's better to catch the product life cycle as it's starting to level off. Then, you basically have three choices:

Reinvent and call it new.

There's something about holding a product that's supposed to solve something, and it boldly states "new" on the label. Like magnets, we tend to be attracted to those products. The marketplace loves large claims, and we seek to prove them. Marketing relies on the power of new. If attendance is waning for a church service that was once popular, I would suggest developing an all-new format to attract others. Be careful, though, as most church leaders will call something "all-new" when the audience views it as very similar to the last failing product. If you use "new," and it's not truly new, you'll lose the power of new in the future. A mid-week prayer meeting that has fallen to very few attendees probably will not grow if you rename it to "Our *New* Prayer Hour" and continue to do similar things during the event.

If you're old enough, you may remember the debacle of New Coke in the mid-80s. It failed because of the backlash of nostalgia. This is when the brand loyalty of the "old" creates a resistance to "new." Through taste tests, Coca-Cola had data to prove that people would prefer the new taste, but they forgot that a certain nostalgia to a brand would create an uproar. For that reason, New Coke failed.

A church needs to be cautious because we don't want to change anything that is clearly established Biblically or strongly nostalgic for our audiences. Otherwise, "new" could possibly kill a great creative idea.

Communicate improvements.

You've probably seen an "improved formula" sticker on clothing detergent. Tide has improved its formula 22 times in its first 21 years on the market.[2] Procter and Gamble realize that the word "improved" can have a similar impact as "new" on a product.

Every ministry product formulation needs to be tested regularly to make sure you're meeting the needs and expectations of your group. Churches are notorious for doing everything the same way with most improvements unnoticed or so incremental that they are ignored. This isn't a problem unless you see a leveling off of satisfaction for the product. Then, you must solve your audience's needs in a much better way, making sure you highlight the improvements. Be sure to explain your conscientiousness and purposeful action. People love that you're watching and making changes to help them. Remember our discussion about *change* in Chapter Four!

Increase audience potential.

If market saturation seems to be the issue, you need to change or increase your audience. This is done better gradually than drastically. Monitor demographic changes that affect your product, and adapt as quickly as possible. If demographics of your communities (inside and/or outside) shift dramatically, you may need to uproot totally and move to a better location. This can be costly, but it's also costly to fail and close your doors.

As I suggested earlier, create a "win" with a small audience, and using that momentum, target another audience segment while being careful not to grow too quickly. Remember that audiences are fickle and can quickly change preferences, so monitor the loyalty of your audience regularly.

Again, let me restate that I'm not recommending that any church do anything outside of the bounds of Scripture. True creativity is not doing whatever it takes to be perceived as different. Instead, it's working inside the bounds of established rules and restrictions, including government regulations, laws, community restrictions, and clearly God's laws.

The "way we've always done it" that exists in communities of faith is not healthy. The Bible doesn't say we must have a prayer service on Wednesday evenings. I understand why we do, though. What better way to encourage your congregation between Sundays! Someone chose the mid-week timeframe and talked about the importance of prayer and fellowship halfway between our main gathering times. It's a perfect time to share our needs and enjoy getting together again as well as a way to watch the power that manifests through a committed prayer time.

The problem is that, for many churches, attendance for this prayer service has long since flattened, and the decline has overtaken it. Few want to change it. The North American Church has attached its folklore to Biblical truth, and when something fails, it appears that the congregation is breaking a Biblical commandment. We need to examine our methods while maintaining the Biblical message. I believe God wants us to take risks with our methods so we can attract and build for the Kingdom. We need to monitor the pulse of our audiences while developing our products. We're called to be fishers of men, but some of us are casting our nets in desert areas and wondering why our fishing is failing. The water dried up a long time ago.

The Bible doesn't talk about the way we should dress in church, the type of music we should use, the color of carpets, the length of service, nor when or if an offering should occur. Should I continue with that list? I'm sure many things come to mind. Instead, the Bible says we should want to get together regularly with other believers to exhort each other. And we should be so concerned about the end times that it would motivate us to get together even more (Heb. 10:24).

Let's be known for a product called "church" that eliminates anything that's perceived as a barrier between us and our external communities.

Discussion #9

List all our ministries. Yes. All of them.

Do they meet the criteria for good ministries? Here they are again:

- Meet needs
- Unique
- Available
- Memorable
- Consistent

How about... are they well-attended? Attendance usually is a good indication of whether a ministry is meeting needs or being communicated properly. Which is it?

Which ones need to be reinvented? How?

Which ones need to be stopped? How?

What would our personas say about our ministries?

How should we approach these change suggestions with our leadership? Our congregation?

Want additional information, downloads, and worksheets? Join us at www.beknownbook.com.

10
KNOW YOUR BENEFIT

You've done everything correctly. You've pinpointed a small, targeted audience, discovered as much as possible about them and have perfected a product for them. But it's still not enough!

We know stories of products that have failed, and only once the product disappeared did people realize how the product could have helped them.

I can name many failed products but not because of the lack of audience or the quality of the product provided. McDonald's Arch Deluxe (or McPizza), Microsoft Zune, Crystal Pepsi, Lawn Darts, MySpace (the old one), Segways, etc. So how did they fail? A lot of money was used to get us to buy these things. But they didn't do well.

Somehow, in their quest to develop an audience and a product, they didn't communicate the intersection between the two. Failing to do so will not bode well.

If, as a church, we create quality products (ministries, events, services, etc.) and we have a congregation and community nearby, we can't simply let the audience know *about* products, or we will fail.

As this chart shows, we must understand where the intersection occurs between the two in order for a message to connect. And that's our place of engagement:

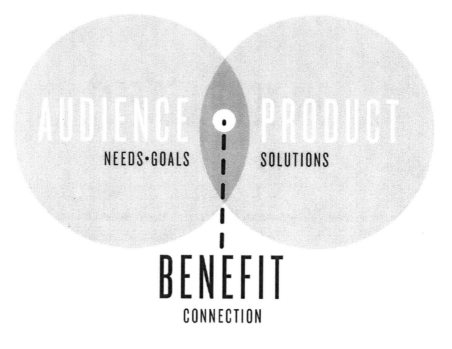

It's essential to connect your product's features to its audience's needs or goals because features alone will rarely sell, attract, or promote. Seldom will an audience grow by virtue of feature awareness. And yet, it's so tempting to try.

The average person loves to talk about the features of a new product, and our churches do it, too...

- "We have plenty of parking!"
- "Our Sunday school classes are so good!"
- "Our choir sings so well!"
- "We have a new app!"
- "We have a pastor for every age group!"

Stop it. Just stop.

The problem? This approach requires the audience to make the connection between the feature and the solution or benefit to them. To be known for features requires extra work from your audience.

In the '70s and '80s, every salesperson was trained in the art of what they called the "elevator pitch." We'd press the button to call the elevator and awkwardly stand with others while waiting for the doors to open. Once we got in, pressed our number, and kindly took requests from everyone else in the small room, we'd nod a salutation. Then, if we got a friendly response, we'd engage. Inevitably, questions about occupation would ensue. We only had about 30 seconds to share what we could in hopes that a business card request would happen.

The savvy salesperson would use such opportunities to talk about value proposition (and not features of their occupation). In the industry, we called it a "unique selling proposition (USP)." It was the one thing that made their product or service uniquely needed. In order to raise interest, they'd simply share the rare benefit. There was no time to list the features of their product in the half minute, so they wanted to get the person's attention as quickly as possible.

It worked.

Today, our attention span is now reduced to even shorter periods of time. If we state features, it will require the audience to identify what solution we're trying to provide through the features, decide if it's needed, and then convert all of this knowledge into understanding of a benefit they'd enjoy.

Most people won't take the time to go through this process, so the message becomes useless information and is quickly forgotten. Because most people make decisions based on what's good for them, people will ignore the entire message if it's not presented with clear benefits.

People make choices to adopt a product based on what they'll receive in return—that is, the solution or benefit. So the local church has to become known for what our benefits and solutions are.

Give people a compelling benefit, and you'll force them to make a yes-or-no decision quickly rather than "what's really in it for me?" You've already told them!

This formula isn't difficult when you truly know your audience and understand you have a product that solves or eases their predominant pains and notable needs. You simply connect the product's features to the audience's benefits when they express interest.

You need to do all of this as quickly as possible. In school, geometry taught us that the shortest distance between two points is a straight line. In marketing communications, the fastest decision-line between your audience and a product is the benefit.

So, how can you make the conversion from a list of features to a benefit? It'll take a little time to work the formula, but it will become easier as you start thinking this way. It'll just happen.

After more than 30 years of working with clients, I have come to realize that most clients love communicating features when they excitedly share about their interesting and unique new product. They share every little detail of the product, and they're truly convinced that people will be as intrigued with the product's features as much as they are. Want an example of this? Simply listen to most stage announcements during any average church service. We try to get all the details out and never really talk about the benefit of going. It often happens something like this:

> Remember the second-annual family picnic is this Saturday on the lawn beside the gym at 11. Try to be a bit early so we can start on time. Please bring a picnic lunch enough for each of you. Soft drinks will be supplied by the church. Bring desserts to share. Everyone is welcome. For more details, go to the church website.

No wonder very few ever remember the events after the announcement time.

The Conversion: Features to Benefits

Features of Products
(that directly correspond to your audience's needs or goals)
in light of your
Audience's Emotional Impact =
Communicated Benefits
(true engagement with your audience)

Here's a step-by-step method to work this conversion:

List your prominent features.

This is the fun part. Simply think about every feature that your church has. I like brainstorming about this with a group. Different features can be identified from different ministry vantage points. When I'm standing in front of a white board and listing the various features identified by a leadership team, there are often many important discussions that occur which help the group to identify other features. This step is eye-opening and interesting. Try to capture all the features so you will have a full understanding of your product. You'll be surprised at how many you'll come up with!

Think about your audience's problem or goals that correspond with each of the features.

Next to each feature, list a problem it solves or a goal it helps. This may be challenging because, often, the feature solves more than one thing. Remember to use the lens of your primary or secondary personas. It's *their* need or pain... not yours.

Assign an emotional response to each solution.

Once you have identified the audience's problem, think about the emotional response your audience might have from receiving the solution—or, at least, the response you want them to have. Here's a list of human emotions to consider[3]:

Acceptance	Embarrassment	Loneliness
Affection	Euphoria	Love
Aggression	Forgiveness	Paranoia
Ambivalence	Frustration	Pity
Apathy	Gratitude	Pleasure
Anxiety	Grief	Pride
Boredom	Guilt	Rage
Compassion	Hatred	Regret
Confusion	Hope	Remorse
Contempt	Horror	Shame
Depression	Hostility	Suffering
Doubt	Homesickness	Sympathy
Ecstasy	Hunger	
Empathy	Hysteria	
Envy	Interest	

But a University of New Glasgow study published in *Current Biology* (and discussed in *Time Magazine*[4]) suggests that we may only have four basic biological emotions:

- Happy
- Sad
- Afraid/surprised
- Angry/disgusted

So if the long list scares you, start with the shorter list of four.

Why is this so important? It will help you to articulate the benefit by understanding the emotional result of your product.

Remember from Chapter One about *choices* that people tend to make decisions based on emotions rather than logic. If you understand the emotional outcome, you can help people to picture the true benefit of what you're offering. Show the benefit in pictures on your website or other communication materials. (More about that later in the book.)

Think what the audience would say if asked, "Why do I need this?"

Look back over your list of features—which has grown to three columns now: features, emotions, and benefits—and think about your primary or secondary personas. Consider how the discussion would go if you asked your audience why they keep coming back to you. This reply should give you a compelling "be known for something" reason for that persona. This would be a great time to conduct a focus group and hear from them directly! You may be surprised.

Order the features in order of perceived priority.

Narrow your list by considering the most compelling features and benefits of what you offer. These would be the ones you do best, the ones that are the rarest (unique), the ones with the most emotional pull, and the ones that are closely associated with basic needs (see Maslow's Hierarchy of Needs in Chapter 8).

Remember that inside the heart of every person is the basic need to discover one's self-worth and purpose in life. Therefore, discovering a relationship with God is high on that list. It's for that reason that you shouldn't shy away from helping someone to know God. At first, they may not quickly engage on such a deep level, but you can certainly introduce it along the way!

Once you have the reduced list of features, consider which ones would be greatly missed by your audience if you removed them. The discussion about this is highly useful, so allow your group (if you're doing it with several people) to discuss this openly. Identify the top two or three features, people's emotional reactions to them, and how people benefit from them.

From those top choices, you should be able to create a unique selling benefit (a be-known-for-something statement), something you could say in one quick sentence that would compel someone to ask, "I want that, but how do you do that?" As soon as someone gets to this question, you have a compelling understanding of your key benefits.

Your stage announcement about the family picnic then becomes...

> Want to meet families like yours from our church and community? This Saturday at 11, let's get together for food and fun! Bring a picnic lunch with desserts to share. We'll supply soft drinks. More details on our website.

It's almost 40 percent shorter but is more compelling because you're leading with the benefit. The features become secondary, and they can find that information on your website.

For example, here are features with well-defined benefits:

Feature	Benefit
Multiple church services	"I can easily attend church when I want."
Lots of free parking	"I don't have to worry about walking a long distance."
Amazing music	"I'm not distracted during worship."
Pastors for every age group	"Our church supports each family member."
Small groups throughout the week	"I can do Bible study when it's convenient."

Now, let's discuss the broader question of "what *should* your church be known for." This becomes more challenging. You must discover and communicate that benefit thread that unites all of your church's events, programs, and features. It should unify and not divide a congregation as well as truly engage your greater community at a deep, emotional level.

Try to word the benefit in the voice of your primary or secondary personas. How would they fill in the blank here? "I attend my church because I _____."

Once you have all your church benefits listed with the items edited and prioritized as discussed, you're ready to discover what you should be known for. So, let's finish the process!

Discussion #10

List all our church's features.

Convert the features to benefits (keeping our personas in mind).

What are the top three or four, based on our personas' preferences?

Want additional information, downloads, and worksheets? Join us at www.beknownbook.com.

II

DISCOVER YOUR THREAD

From the discussion about the three simple things (audience, product, and benefit) process, I hope you've done enough self-reflection and corporate soul-searching to realize whether you're currently known for the right things. Or, maybe, you're ready to lock down a better thread. The effort is worth it.

Getting the correct thread will reconnect you to your community and motivate them to pay attention, listen, and engage with your ministries and messages.

Revitalizing and controlling your church's reputation (your thread!) will allow you to be known for something incredibly valuable to people who need it.

Ready to continue the process and nail your thread down?

As a review of where you should be along the process, a highly effective be-known-something thread should exhibit the qualities we discussed in Chapter Three:

- It needs to be simple. 1-5 words. Memorable.
- It needs to be emotionally charged.
- It needs to be benefit-driven. From your audience's perspective.

- It needs to feel like your congregation. And your community.
- It needs to be unique. The rarer, the better.
- It needs to be ambiguous (so you can extend it).

It's certainly not your vision or mission statement, but it should run parallel to its meaning and be your audience's emotional response to watching your mission playing out. They would want to tell those in their community who need the benefit.

Because it's intended for people who haven't committed to a church or to Christ, think in a non-religious sense. But make sure it can make the turn to Jesus quite easily.

This thread statement can become your greatest evangelism tool for your church. When someone in your community hears it, they should be compelled to attend, engage, or at least ask, "How do you deliver that?"

It should be positive yet easily connected to a prominent need in the community or a path to a goal.

Enough review... Here's how our team discovers a thread for one of our clients. You can do it, too.

Your thread must grow from your personas and their concerns, problems, and goals. See Chapter Eight for those details.

In your mind, become those personas as if you're playing a great role-playing game. Think like them.

In case you've forgotten, review your chart of features, benefits, and emotions from Chapter Ten.

Make sure you've prioritized the list so that the most important benefits are at the top. This can be achieved by thinking about the persona and imagining what would be that person's most emotional reaction. Or, think about what would solve the largest nagging concern in their lives. Or, figure out what would take them on an important path to a crucial goal.

Decide where the cut-off will be. Perhaps the top five or the top ten? Usually, it becomes obvious on the list, based on validity.

Start brainstorming taglines and statements based on those benefits. Get the help of a wordsmith, if necessary. Write down as many ideas as possible that work with the benefits of your church.

Occasionally, other ideas that work with your personas will come to mind. Write them down, too! No ideas are wrong at this stage.

The more you brainstorm, the more you'll get the hang of it. Sometimes, we end up with 40 or 50 threads that can work.

Now, put on your judge's robes and eliminate any that can't be extended across all your ministries.

Consider editing each thread further. Eliminate words or concepts. While doing this, see if more spring up from your list. While we eliminate, we often add more. Sometimes, we end up with more in our elimination process!

Now, eliminate any that sound corny, contrived, too churchy, not relevant, too obscure, or that just don't work.

Bring the leadership team back together who started this journey if they haven't been part of the brainstorming. For sure, you should involve the senior leadership of your church and anyone who will want to use the thread.

Present the foundation again about personas and benefits to get their heads back into the mindset again. Present the ideas you've come up with.

Ask for input and preference. One (or more) will usually rise to the top.

You've discovered your thread.

Congratulations! The next few chapters will describe how you can communicate it so you become known for it.

Examples

We have helped hundreds of churches with these branding principles. And usually, at this point, the church leaders say, "Give us some examples, please, so we can understand better."

I'm always reticent to do that.

My fear is that, if I give examples from other churches, the churches I'm talking with will simply copy the outcome of hundreds of hours of research and creativity that went into someone else's threads. Also, their threads are directly related to *their* own communities in which God has placed them. One thread will not work effectively in all communities.

But I also would like to demonstrate some good threads. And I'd like to reward you for buying this book and reading this far! Please, though, realize these are not to be copied and applied to your brand. You need to have a genuine thread rise-up from your community and speak about the product your church is delivering.

Some ideas for effective threads:

- Acceptance. Here.
- Honest Discussion
- You're Not Alone.
- Finish Strong.

When you see a good thread, you should be able to identify the personas a church is targeting as well as what the church wants as its key benefit and the understood problem to which they are providing a solution.

Here are a couple of threads incorporated into the visual brand and a brief explanation of why and how the church is effectively weaving the thread through all of their communication materials.

Client: First Baptist Church Jonesboro (near Atlanta)

Reach area: What was once a predominantly Caucasian area has now become diversified with a vibrant population of many ethnicities. Rather than settling for their historically, mainly-white congregation, the dynamic ministry leaders chose to reach out to everyone in the community... to share the love of Christ with all people and truly do "Life. Together."

Thread concept with visual brand: Paths crisscross as life is conducted together with others, creating a mosaic that represents a diverse community doing business, enjoying leisure time, and exploring their spiritual side. The cross that appears within the symbol demonstrates their core belief that, through Christ's sacrificial death on the cross, we are able to do "Life. Together." Think community, life, work, and church has to be divided? Think again. This is the place that brings "Life. Together."

Why a circle? Because there are no "corners" in their ministries. Together, life unfolds in the openness of conversation and transparency found within the teachings of Scripture.

This contemporary symbol also represents the traditional stain-glassed windows that adorn their beautiful buildings. The hand-script of their thread tagline demonstrates a personalization of the benefit offered at this church. We... can do *Life. Together.*

Website: www.fbcjonesboro.com

More to Life.

Client: Kingwood United Methodist Church (near Houston)

Reach area: This booming area outside the metropolis of the hustling city of Houston has become an upscale oasis for retired, oil-rich families and optimistic, dreaming families seeking a better life in the oil industry and associated business sectors. The area is rich with great people, great stories, growing families, growing businesses, and a wonderful overgrowth of tall trees and protected natural areas.

Thread concept with visual brand: For those seeking refuge after a busy career where the pursuit of wealth has left them exhausted, Kingwood UMC gives solace and understanding that there's "More to Life" than the pursuits they've chased.

For the younger and established families in the area who have one or more parents busy with challenging work, this dynamic place of worship brings the family together and balances their achievements with a spiritual perspective. Yes, there *is* "More to Life."

The leaves in their simple symbol, forming the representative "K", embody the abundance of tree overgrowth surrounding their campus but also demonstrate the potential growth that can occur when you recognize there's truly "More to Life" than the busyness of occupational goals.

Website: www.kingwoodumc.org

Discussion #11

Does our thread meet all the qualities of a good thread?

Do we all like the direction? What if some of us don't? How will we deal with that?

The true test? What will our personas think? Will it be a benefit they'll want to come and get?

Want additional information, downloads, and worksheets? Join us at www.beknownbook.com.

Part 4

BE FOUND

12

COMMUNICATING YOUR SOMETHING

By this chapter, I'm assuming you have your thread—or, at least, that you've reduced your list to very few that could work. This is exciting! But your thread isn't going to grow your church or unite your ministries unless you start communicating it outside of the leadership team that helped discover it. And that's the hard part.

How does industry communicate something new? I, of course, think about Apple who is a master at it.

I remember my first smartphone. Being an early adopter, especially with electronics, I've usually taken the risk to get a reward. I still liked my clamshell-style phone when the rumored first iPhone was bantered about back in 2007. The small phone easily fit into my pocket, made it easy to make and take calls, and actually had a calculator and an address book! I thought I had it all.

Then, in Apple fashion, Steve Jobs stood in front of a small audience and launched his new device. He was so good at unveiling things. We didn't realize how much we needed them until we watched his presentations. With evangelistic fervor, he would get us excited with the company, making sure we were happy to associate ourselves with the Apple brand. Then, as excitedly as possible, he'd explain the pain of what we had been dealing with regularly. He would say things along the lines of, "Can you imagine having to get your emails on your computer, which kept you tethered to your office?" "Why should you have to carry a phone in your pocket or on your hip all while having an iPod with you while you were away from your office or vehicle?" "Imagine being able to converge everything into a cool-looking device that would sync everything for your every whim." And then, with childlike fascination, he would demonstrate the new device as if he was figuring it out in front of all of us. It was pure genius. We "caught" the Apple delight, realizing we could also have that excitement, and we didn't have to be concerned about a learning curve. After all, we reasoned, even Steve figured it out in front of us! It was exactly what the technology industry needed, a just-in-time solution communicated flawlessly.

Apple identified its audience, reminded us of our concerns, and presented us something we'd benefit from.

You've now followed the be-known-for-something process and know who your two audiences are (congregation and community). You know their pains and goals (perhaps, even before they do!), and you know the one benefit you want to be known for. That's the hard part, condensing everything you are down to a communication thread that will resonate.

Now what? There are three ways to become known for your be-known-for-something thread:

1: Let people catch on to it.

Because you genuinely deliver the benefit you talk about and because you "are" the solution, people around you will start to understand and want your solution. And when people discover a solution, they talk about it, share it, and promote it... much like the moment when I got my first iPhone. I showed everyone what it could do and tried selling its benefits to all my friends.

This is an inexpensive way to accomplish your communication but is incredibly slow. Word-of-mouth communication relies on meeting people one by one, making sure they understand who you are and what you should be known for. It usually takes time for people to become your promoter. And in the meantime, others could possibly copy what you're known for by hearing your message. However, the more compelling and unique you are, the faster you will gain traction. But it will still happen excruciatingly slow.

2: Communicate it everywhere.

There are many ways to do this. You can individually walk around and tell people. You can hire a communications team to do it. You can convince volunteers to talk to everyone they know. But doing it verbally is only slightly better than the first option. Instead, you need to look at all communication opportunities (i.e. social, print, web, etc.) and use as many as you can afford and have time for.

3: Do a combination.

This is the solution. It's the most time-effective, cost-effective, and proactive way to become known for something. Let's look at ways to effectively communicate your thread.

Brand Foundation

Establish a complete brand. You're almost there. You have a great be-known-for-something thread, but you need more.

Logo

We are a visual people, so we will usually remember a visual cue faster and longer than abstract words. The problem is we see a ton of advertising images. According to a Yankelovich Marketing Agency study in 2007, a person living in an urban center sees about 5,000 marketing messages daily (as compared to only 2,000 just three decades earlier).[5] I'm sure we've had even further increases in the years since. We love to "see" what we believe in! Because of the huge barrage of images in our view, we must raise our standard in order to compete with anyone else who's trying to get the attention of others. Your logo is a good place to start.

First, it needs to be simple. If a seventh-grader can't draw it from memory, it's probably too complex. Don't add unnecessary complexity in an effort to add a "deeper" spiritual message. In fact, your logo doesn't have to have religious symbolism in it at all. Not having a cross, dove, crown, flames, etc. does not affect your spirituality! A logo shouldn't tell people what you do. It should simply be a unique, easy-to-remember symbol that associates you with your brand promises. What you wear doesn't make you a Christian; it just lets you have a style. Also, a simple logo can be used at any size necessary (maintaining readability) as well as for any usage (e.g. digital, embroidery, print, etc.).

It doesn't need to be clever. We have clients request "clever" regularly. That's a difficult word. I think they want a hidden meaning behind the logo. Instead of seeking some magic in your logo, you should seek professionalism. If clever happens in the process, it's an added bonus.

It needs to stand up to what the world is offering. As believers, we have a better "product." This isn't just your local church and what it has to offer; this is Jesus, the solution to every need! He's better than anything the world has to offer, so we need to create a brand wrapper that's better than we typically do in our local churches. We're called to a higher standard than what the secular world has to offer!

Take a look at the current logos of elite companies. They've been thoroughly thought out and well-designed. Yes, there's a reason for each element, and the elements are balanced. Many professional hours have been devoted to developing it. So, stop getting a kid, neighbor, novice, secretary, or sub-standard alternative to design your logo. Your logo is one of the best investments you can purchase. Everything will be built on its foundation, and the wise man builds his house on a solid foundation.

After decades of creating logos for clients (secular and ministry), I want to issue several additional areas of caution as well as a few recommendations concerning logo design.

Resist getting opinions about the logo from people who didn't have initial input. I'm amazed by how often the following scenario occurs. We have our initial exploratory meeting with a client and decide on a general direction. We work for hours on ideas. That process isn't easy. We discuss it internally, sharing what we heard in our input meeting and get rough sketches of concepts. An art or creative director then narrows down the ideas based upon experience of what will work well for a solid, unique brand. Then, the designers clean up the designs in a vector program. Usually, at this stage, we still have too many to present, so we eliminate based on our professional wisdom. We will need to work with the logo later as the brand expands, so we know which designs will be easiest to build on. Finally, we present three or four final concepts to the client that represent many years of expertise. The client thanks us for our work. In a few days, we get feedback that the secretary or the pastor's wife really doesn't like any of them.

The people who are going to be making the final decision *must* be present in the initial meetings. If not, you'll end up paying for extra revisions and frustrate the creatives in the process. If you're truly using professionals, you should get professional work that can be tied directly to your initial thoughts, goals, and strategy. Don't quickly throw away their ideas.

Don't overcomplicate this process. The process is clear. The client provides direction, and we assist with shaping that direction, supplying logo selections with the client loving one or two of them. Everyone's happy. But occasionally, the client overcomplicates the process by overthinking. It's like going clothes shopping with a friend or spouse, and *nothing* seems to fit or be their style. Can it truly be that way? Of course, not. Instead, their expectations are far too high, or they want something that no self-respecting designer would produce. There's nothing worse than settling... for us or for the client.

Look at a portfolio of design work that has been created by your designer. Make sure you love his or her style at that stage. Make sure they love the Church and have worked with a local church before. In the initial meeting, make sure they understand what you want to be known for. There should be a synergy and connection. You should trust your designer to produce work that you'll like... a simple, professional logo that is unique and memorable in your community. Don't overthink every aspect of it.

When it comes to logo styles, it gets complicated. Your logo needs to match your church's style. Most churches can't easily change their architecture. So when a traditional church requests a contemporary logo, we could end up with a brand disconnect. You may attract with a contemporary logo, but they'll be turned off by the traditional, old-style building that they drive up to.

The solution? Start with what can't or won't change. These parameters establish creative fences that will allow the designers to play safely within. Think about other limitations, and realize that your brand must work within their style.

Don't get me wrong; creating a logo that's modern yet still balanced with your limitations can be done. You'll want the brand style to match the non-changeable things you can't change easily. If you insist on a contemporary look, you can create a brand that is on the contemporary side of traditional. If you insist on a very contemporary look, you're risking looking inauthentic.

And people (especially Millennials) will see through that immediately, jeopardizing the integrity of your entire ministry.

Where do the words go? There are typically two kinds of logos: ones that are mainly stylized words (wordmarks) and ones that are stylized words with a logo symbol. Both are fine for churches; however, your stylized words need to represent your church thread, which is difficult. If you have a long name, I'd say don't do it. If you do go this route, ensure that the words are stylized with a unique font that you can own for your brand. For most churches, however, we recommend a symbol that can be used apart from the words. It does a few things.

First, it will allow a personality to emerge. When you only have a font to work with, you're somewhat limited for uniqueness, personality, and message. A symbol will enable you to create something that works with your selected font and creates a holistic feel for your church.

Design flexibility: Being able to use a component or style from your symbol in other designs (or brand extensions) is huge for your brand. Because your logo should be on everything you communicate, it will start to reinforce your brand and will allow your family of materials to grow from your symbol. This gives you more to work with than just a font in a wordmark.

Horizontal vs. vertical logo: When I started doing brand creation, print material was the driving force behind all communications. Now, the focus is on online communications. So, design decisions need to be made based on limitations of website design. The trend right now with websites is to make the header area — the graphics area containing your logo, search bar, etc. at the top of the website page — is growing narrower and narrower. As it compresses, it doesn't leave room for a tall, vertical logo, so you'll need a horizontal logo more than likely. This doesn't mean you can't have a vertical logo (symbol on top with words under it). It just means you need another version of it that's horizontal (symbol to the left with words to the right). Be careful when you have two versions of a logo, though, so it doesn't fragment a strong and consistent brand.

Be-known-for-something thread/statement: Most non-profits don't have a large communication budget. So, unlike large national brands who advertise broadly, you will need to make every communication purchase work hard. Because your be-known-for-something thread represents your attractive benefit and *is* what you want to be known for, I would suggest that you create a logo that has the statement incorporated near it. That way, if the logo is used, the statement will be associated with it and will remind everyone about what you're known for. Make sure it's large enough so it will be readable when small versions of the logo are used, but the statement should never overpower the logo. The visual (the logo) should lead, and the statement should be secondary. When pushing your core benefit/solution (especially at the beginning of establishing the brand), we often recommend "leading" with the be-known-for-something statement as the headline. When doing that, we don't overkill the communication with a logo *and* the statement.

Color Palette

I see someone regularly, and she's always nicely dressed. One day when I ran into her, there was something totally different about her. I asked if she had gotten a haircut and stopped short, asking if she'd dyed her hair another shade. As we talked, I continued to question other things about her internally. Had she lost weight? Had a nose job? It was driving me crazy. Then, I realized that she almost always wore black or dark tones. That day, she was in a fuchsia, floral outfit. She seemed wildly different.

As an organization, you need to decide what "clothes" you'll be wearing as you promote your church. Color, therefore, becomes part of your brand. How much color should be in your brand? There's a 60/30/10 color rule in interior design: 60% of your design should consist of a predominant color, 30% should consist of another color, and 10% would be a sparing splash of another color. I like to think it's similar to wearing a suit. The jacket and pants (or skirt) are usually one primary color, the shirt is a secondary color, and the tie (or scarf) is usually a pop of color in the middle of everything. That balance has become widely accepted, so your brand needs that balance, too.

When we enjoy a brand promise (thread) and experience the same color combination while doing it, we start to associate the combination with the benefit. It's part of the overall experience. So, consistently use your three colors, occasionally using other coordinating colors as part of your suite of colors. Become known for them! Subliminally, many brands do this.

When you walk into a Staples office supply store, Best Buy, or McDonald's restaurant, notice how they use their color palette everywhere, using other colors only to enhance the "suite." Under the "golden arches," you'll find golds coupled with just enough crimson red. Best Buy balances yellow, blues, and black. And at Staples, you'll see how they coordinate their Retail Red with white and yellow.

The large retailers and brands know that they want to be recognized. Stand out and look consistent to appear consistent in delivery of a benefit. It works. You can be in a store and know where you are without seeing a logo.

For your church, you don't want to look like a retail store or massive branding guru, but your colors need to follow the same principles based on how much branding you want to be evident. Your logo and signage may boast your colors while your other decor has a coordinating, "interior-decorated" appearance. Just ensure that everything coordinates well and is maintained consistently. Many church worship rooms have a main color, so I would suggest, if possible, that you incorporate that into your palette or consider changing the worship center color.

Because certain colors are trendy and become dated quickly, I would suggest (like good interior decorators suggest) that you use non-trendy colors (black or neutral) on things that are costly to change. You can always re-paint a focus wall easily as color trends change. When it comes to your color suite, though, I'd suggest that your primary and secondary colors not be too trendy.

You can change the tertiary (tie/scarf color) occasionally without changing your overall brand.

Like a professionally tailored suit, there are certain colors that shouldn't be worn as a suit. The same applies for most shirts. But a tie is where you can have fun! A well-selected tie can change an average suit into a runway favorite. And because the suit costs the most, you wouldn't want to change it continuously. Here is a color principle to protect your brand: have fun with a pop (tertiary) color if you'd like, but don't go crazy or trendy with your primary or secondary colors!

I met with a pastor recently about color. We started talking about decorating his church. His frustration bubbled up. "Why is it always a committee of people who can barely decorate their own homes that take the lead in interior decorating for our churches?" He's right. Your brand should feel like a well-designed home. There are few branded stores that you'd want to live in, but they seem right as a store and have convinced us that we, as their persona, feel at home in their locations.

I've been in the Headquarters of L.L. Bean in Maine, and because I love the outdoors and nature excursions that they promote, I love the ambience, the thought, and the inspiration that they bring to the purchasing experience. I feel like I could live in their flagship store. Why? It enhances the shopping experience and makes me feel comfortable about purchasing something. With a brand, everything is controlled. Merchandisers subtly aide in the purchase decision, placing the right things in the right locations to move someone through the store. At L.L. Bean, they do this while subtly wrapping the L.L. Bean brand everywhere.

A church needs to have professional help to get the balance right. You need to determine what your needs and requirements are for your building. And then, more importantly, you must decide how your brand will expand into the feeling of the building and worship experience. Don't simply copy other churches in what they're doing or the latest trend. Be original for your brand thread, and fulfill the expectations and satisfaction of your audience.

It seems like churches love to copy one another. When I was growing up, our family would vacation and travel regularly. It was never a question of whether we would pack church clothes. We always did. And we always attended local churches. Many were small, one-room churches with lots of wood furnishings, and many in Atlantic Canada at the time had a central aisle between rows of rock-hard wooden pews. In the center of aisle, one would often find a wood stove that was stoked before (and sometimes during) the service.

Then, there were the modern churches that didn't have cathedral ceilings but had a contemporary flair with flat ceilings. Almost every one of them had white or cream walls, oak trim, and dark-colored carpeting that coordinated with the bold pew padding.

Now, as I continue to visit churches across the country, modern worship centers seem to be trending toward black walls, black exposed ceilings, and chairs that are comfortable like fine theatre seats. I've often wondered what church was the first to do it. There had to be one! Someone came up with this idea to tone everything down around the room (black) so the rest of the room would become almost invisible so our focus would be on the worship being presented under the stage lights. I guess it copied the secular stage experience, but one church decided to start the trend. And because it made sense, it caught on. Now, many are doing it.

What if your brand created a look and feel that became the next trend... and years from now, we'll all wonder who the first was? This usually doesn't come from a committee of nice people in your congregation. And because it costs so much to do it right, it needs to be well-considered, so I'd recommend using architectural designers or retail interior decorators who understand the church world.

Everything speaks. If you're trying to be known for your thread, your benefit, think about the emotion that comes from experiencing it, and ensure that feeling envelops the entire campus of your church with your colors. It's more than painting a focus wall. If your benefit evokes a strong feeling of joy, as you walk through your facility, you need to make sure that joy exudes from everywhere. Everywhere in your building, there should be something (your thread) that proclaims you're about joy, something (a color combination or hint of your logo or design) that assures everyone that they are part of your brand story. Stop creating totally separate, disjointed environments that feel like different brands. Or, at the least, we need to have some connective branding threads that tie the sub-brands to your master brand.

Also, remember that interior decorating goes through trends faster than most other things. A good sofa should endure regular use for a dozen years, but often, people buy a new sofa every 3-5 years. Why? Because we tend to tire of what's around us, and the furniture industry accelerates trends to induce sales. Anticipate that your ministry leaders will suggest changing the decorating and brand in a facility.

This doesn't usually come from the congregation, though. It's usually from staff and leadership who experience 60-hour workweeks around it (compared to the 3-5 hours per week that the average member does). Be careful not to change for the sake of change. Experts will help you to create ways to establish longevity of colors, textures, and styles.

Are you ready for a change in brand color, though? Your branding color suite shouldn't change complete hues when "updating" the brand palette. In other words, if you have a blue, beige, and green palette; you can shift your colors slightly to use a more trendy blue, beige, or green without killing all the brand equity you've achieved through your colors.

Your marketing communication materials should also maintain a strong, consistent color palette. You shouldn't be stumped with "what color should we use?" when it comes to ads, the website, e-blasts, brochures, etc. Always start with your color palette so that, when your audience see the complete body of communication materials, there will be a consistency of colors. This adds value and recall to your brand.

Font Palette

The same can be said for your fonts. If you consistently control the fonts you use, it will be easier, cheaper, and more brand-empowering. There are basically two "types" of fonts: ones with serifs and ones without (sans-serif). A serif was established with hand-lettering many centuries ago. The calligrapher would start the ink in his pen by swiping left and right to put an extension on most strokes. People became used to reading this style, so as printing presses and typography started developing, they added the serifs because people liked them. Research has shown that people use the serifs to read paragraphs more easily by allowing the eye to glide along the lines of text and helping people to read faster.

Because web is taking the lead in communications now, we've discovered that sans-serif fonts are used pervasively there. A brand using sans-serif feels cleaner and more modern. Using serifs has a more traditional feel.

We'd suggest starting with the fonts in your logo to establish your font palette unless they're not legible when used in paragraph form. It might be wise to incorporate a serif and a sans-serif in your logo to give you options if you're a blended church (traditional and contemporary).

If you only use a serif font in your logo, you'll probably still need a sans-serif as part of your font palette because a sans-serif works better online.

For most churches, you probably need only two fonts for your material: a sans-serif and a serif. You could probably exist with just a sans-serif (if you have a modern brand), but most should have a serif font for print materials (paragraph form) and a sans-serif for online materials. Headlines and subheadings in print form can use either one. If you're using a handwritten script font, as a general rule, it should be limited to headlines or sub-heads for readability.

Caution about Fonts

I visited a church recently whose pastor thought it would be wise to use Comic Sans as one of their fonts. You know, it's that whimsical, "hand-drawn" font that is associated with speech bubbles in comic strips. I asked the pastor why he chose it for his sermon points on the screen. He said, "It just feels so friendly and doesn't feel preachy." True. But it feels unbelievable, too, like there's a punch line coming up. It makes a sermon feel like a stand-up comedy act. Can you tell I don't think there's any place for Comic Sans in the church? (Unless you're a church catering to clowns and comedians, of course.)

Papyrus is another font I'd caution against using, too. Instead, use professional fonts that feel friendly and open but are serious enough to talk about God and the gospel.

All fonts are similar. Each one usually has an uppercase and a lowercase version, and if not, be careful as this would limit their versatility. And each of the 26 letters and 10 numbers are represented with a font type. It's a bonus when the font includes lots of other optional symbols and characters that match the style of the font. In this era of internet symbols, always make sure there's a hashtag (#) included in the font. Back slashes (/) and greater than (<>) symbols come in handy, too. Here are some other things to consider:

Make sure it's readable.

Fonts should communicate. There's nothing worse than when someone says, "What does that say?" If there's *any* letter that doesn't quite read as the right letter, consider not using it. Or if the font (scripts are notorious for doing this) is not readable in a sentence, reconsider the choice.

Make sure your design is not all about the font.

A font should add personality and potentially create a unique feel for your brand. Often, if the font has a huge personality or is too unique, it's too strong for your brand.

Make sure it's "open."

Look at the letter "o" in your font. Studies have shown that the rounder the letter, the more friendly it feels. The more oval-shaped it is, the less "inclusive" it will feel.

Make sure it has good kerning.

Type a sentence with it. Then, look at the spacing between letters (kerning). Does it look even? Or can you see wide, weird spaces between characters? Steer clear. Back when type was hand set for printing, they would add or remove little pieces of wood between letters called a "kern," depending on the letters that were adjacent to them. Thankfully, professional fonts now add that space automatically. If you're constantly having to adjust the kerning (sometimes called letter "spacing") in order to have a professional look, it's not worth the time.

Make sure it's not too expensive.

Good fonts cost money. "What?!" Yes, someone who designs and spends the proper amount of time on a font will usually charge for it. A font foundry is the name of the store that licenses or sells these files. It's wise to check to see if you're using a font for free that you should have paid for. If you need to pay for it (or license it to many people), make sure it won't break your budget.

Make sure there's a web font for it.

You'll probably have to represent your font somehow in a CSS (Cascading Style Sheet) on your website. The easiest thing is to use a font that's very similar (and is included in most systems). For the most part, here they are: Georgia, Palatino Linotype, Book Antiqua, Palatino, Times New Romans, Times, Arial, Helvetica, Arial Black, Comic Sans (ugh), Impact, Charcoal, Lucida Sans Unicode, Lucida Grande, Tahoma, Geneva, Trebuchet MS, Helvetica, Verdana, Geneva, Courier New, Lucida Console, and Monaco. Yes, there are ways to use other fonts like Google Web Fonts (talk to your developer), but these fonts may slow your website down or may not work on all browsers. Just don't use screen captures or images for your web fonts because they usually can't be detected by search engines.

Make sure it's friendly.

Even if you have an open font (as described above), make sure it looks friendly and cheery. Christianity should be known for love, and love is certainly friendly!

Make sure it matches your personality.

Remember the brand personality I keep talking about? You need to make sure that your personality shines through your font. If you use a "regular," easy-to-read font, this doesn't really apply. Because I'm a font connoisseur (snob?), I believe every font has a built-in personality. See below for how fonts add to your design personality palette.

Make sure it is used consistently.

Please. Please. Please. If you have a font palette, please use it consistently. Style sheets are advised. Know when to bold, italicize, or underline text. The way you use it is as important as what font you use. This needs to be understood and shared with anyone who controls your communications.

Avoid all uppercase.

NO ONE LIKES ALL CAPS. Typing that sentence was excruciatingly difficult. Uppercase is no longer seen as emphasis as much as SCREAMING. Just like few preachers scream all the time, we need to communicate by not screaming. Plus, studies have shown that readers tend to run their eyes along the x-height of the line (the top of the lowercase letter) to read quickly. We don't really take in the whole letter. Instead, the x-height gives us most of the information. If you use all uppercase, you eliminate these visual cues, forcing your readers to slow down.

Design Personality

Once you have your logo, colors, and fonts nailed down, your brand personality should be evident. Use your be-known-for-something thread to guide you and ensure your personality is remaining true to the emotional response from your brand. Then, use something in your communications list to "lead" your brand development. This should be either a web design, sign, stationary, brochure, etc. through which your designers can show an extension of the logo, using the colors and fonts.

As we tackle this step, we realize that other design components are needed in order to create the whole brand. These include (but aren't limited to)…

- Amount of white space
- Square corners or round
- Lines (thickness and shape)
- Background patterns
- Borders

In the industry, all of these controlled design elements are called a graphic standard. It's best to write these down to maintain consistency either as a page of information or a booklet of details. This can also be the job of a communications director, art director, or designer to remember it. If you don't control all of these things, you're wasting your time and a bunch of money on redesigning. And, ultimately, you won't have an established brand. You need a consistent visual to point to your thread!

Share your graphic standard with everyone who creates materials for your church, keep it up to date, and review it regularly. Occasionally, you'll want to adapt some of the elements as your brand progresses, but be careful not to be swayed by overly ambitious designers who like to change everything regularly, blaming their whims on boredom.

Again, you will get tired of your brand *long* before your audience will simply because you're working with it consistently while the average person in your congregation sees it randomly throughout the week and on Sundays (if they go each week). Your target audience will only see your brand a few times a year (based upon your budget). I would rather build a strong, consistent brand and risk getting tired of it than to change things randomly, preventing anyone from identifying your brand.

The Ultimate Brand Test

When you have an established, solid brand (the kind that organizations acquire for tons of money when they purchase the "name"), you have something so strong that people will know who's communicating before they see the logo or hear the name. With your logo hidden on something from your church, can someone still instantly know it looks like your brand?

When you see a Gap commercial, almost instantly, you know the stark white backgrounds and blue square "screams" Gap even before the logo appears at the end. Or, if someone blindfolded you, took you inside a McDonald's, and allowed you to look around (even without seeing a logo), you'd recognize the brand. Or in a Walmart. Or a Best Buy.

Lock down consistency.

Our churches are a clearinghouse for random ideas. People could wander inside one of your buildings and forget where they are. Or a visitor could walk away from an initial visit and never remember your brand. Our world expects this professionalism everywhere else. Let's give it to them in the local church!

Discussion #12

Score the following parts of our brand foundation using the information from the chapter (1 = We need to do something about this; 10 = The church world can learn from us)

- Logo
- Color palette
- Font palette
- Design personality
- Our be-known-for-something thread

What are we going to do with any of the ones scoring less than 5?

How can we be more consistent with our brand without over-using it?

Want additional information, downloads, and worksheets? Join us at www.beknownbook.com.

13

REAP THE REWARDS

Being known for something just makes sense. Building that consistent thread into a basic graphic standard manual will allow your brand to be recognizable with top-of-mind awareness from your community. This is when you can fully engage with them and both of you can enjoy the benefits! The community consistently receives the solutions, benefits, and paths to goals that your brand thread promises, but here are some unexpected rewards that *you'll* enjoy:

It'll save time.

When you send your child to a school that requires a school uniform, there are time savings every morning when your child wakes up and has to decide what he or she will wear. And if the school only allows black bottoms and a white button-down shirt, there's not much decision-making needed. Imagine the time that would be saved each day! Having a consistent, locked-down palette for your church will provide similar time savings.

But is it boring? Not at all. There are still many choices that can be made while maintaining a graphic standard. In the school with a uniform, children can still comb their hair as they'd like, choose to wear a jacket, or a girl can wear different makeup for individuality. Though, ultimately, when all the school kids gather for a class picture, it's obvious someone created and maintained school consistency throughout the group.

Church ministries should also be allowed to have individuality with their communications and environments, but they need to know the branding thread and graphic standard that they can't change. Some think it's limiting, but once adopted, it will save decision time and build a strong brand.

It'll save money.

I've worked with designers for decades. In fact, I am one! I know that the heart of a designer loves to discover, explore, create, and be wild. We love the idea of "the sky's the limit!" But in any given project, there are so many decisions that must be made, and every decision takes time. A well-documented graphic standard introduces creative boundaries for them to play within, eliminating some of the decision time. This time savings will allow you to save money if you pay by the hour or get more work from someone who's salaried.

Expect some designers to push back, though. Much like being put into a garden and being told not to eat of one tree, it becomes tempting to push against the limits and continually try to reach for the forbidden fruit. Good designers love exceptions to the rules! Just be clear about what will be acceptable and what won't. Set these clear boundaries early in the process, or a designer will become rebellious... like a person who just found out about a new rule in the middle of a card game. When a designer, secretary, production artist, or volunteer starts a communication piece, they should know acceptable fonts, colors, and branded design parameters from the moment they open the new document on their computer. In fact, because some of these standards will create a base for materials, I'd recommend establishing templates (with style sheets) that will enable production of materials to happen even more quickly and consistently.

It'll eliminate stress.

Once a team understands your graphic standard, knowing certain things aren't debatable, there's a peace and unity that comes from it. Churches have so many communication materials needing to be produced, and most do not have much time to get these tasks done. If you predetermine as many consistent things as possible, it will eliminate the stress of having to create at breakneck speed. When the notorious "quick job" comes in, it should be asked, "What previous project should it be based on?" Once you know that and know acceptable parameters of your brand, it should start calming the people involved in the process. As a church communicator, you'll also start to gain respect because you're directing and guiding a process that can be replicated for other projects.

The goal is to eliminate the rogue, one-of-a-kind, projects that don't build your brand or reinforce your thread. Everything that reaches your congregation and community *must* work together to establish your purpose... what you're known for. When that system and strategy is established and consistently accomplished, your church is a good steward of the resources it's been given.

Discussion #13

How can discovering a thread save us money?

How can it save us time?

How can it reduce stress?

Of these three, describe which is the most important to you right now in our church.

Want additional information, downloads, and worksheets? Join us at www.beknownbook.com.

14

LEARNING FROM THE PAST

Since the creation of mankind, when we've had a message, we've been motivated to share it with others. Inside all of us lives a desire to communicate because we're made in the image of the Great Communicator.

As a church, we need to learn to communicate more effectively. Where better to begin than the Bible?

Spoken word started before the Garden of Eden when God was the first to speak. God said, "Let there be light" (Gen. 1:3). Then, once humans were created on the sixth day (Gen. 1:28), God talked directly to them, commanding them to multiply. God spoke first. Then, men and women have been perfecting our own communications ever since.

People quickly wanted to speak to more than one person at a time, so they gathered family and community groups together to share stories. It's the way early history was passed from generation to generation. Maybe God allowed people to live to very old ages so the overlapping generations could engage and ask questions about what actually happened.

Jesus and others who have spoken to even larger groups throughout history would gather people on hillsides so their voices would be heard.

Yes, we all want our messages to be heard. Consider all humans have done to simplify the communication process!

Handwriting

Languages were written with letters so the masses could read our messages. Manuscripts only survived as long as the substrates they were written on. Papyrus, early paper, didn't last longer than a couple hundred years. So, better paper was invented in the 14th century.

Printing

We can thank Johannes Gutenberg for perfecting the movable-type printing press in 1450. This allowed messages to be duplicated more easily and then be distributed. Books, flyers, and pamphlets became commonplace as printing presses became more popular.

Newspapers

Single-source material gave way to multiple-source material in one easy-to-read document that could be distributed. America got its first newspaper in 1690 (*Publick Occurrences*), which included paid advertisements that allowed for its printing.

Soon, people realized that, without ads, newspapers couldn't survive, so the amount of ads determined the size of the newspaper. A little more than a century later, America had more than 700 newspapers, all communicating and engaging with a specific audience.

Radio

By the end of the 1800s, radio started sweeping the communication world, an invisible way to transmit messages without paper or typesetting. I'm sure the printing industry was scared at the time. KDKA (Pennsylvania) is believed to have been the first commercial radio station in the U.S. (1920). The station used broadcasted presidential election results on its first day. An important message needed to get out!

Television

Shortly after radio, people attempted to transmit images and sound together. A Scottish inventor (Baird) achieved a "live transmission of moving images with continuous tonal variation" in 1925. Then, the first U.S. television service appeared in 1928 with all-electronic, color TVs appearing in the U.S. by 1953. Radio thought it would be replaced.

Internet

Surprisingly, stemming back to the 1950s, this method of communication by connecting computers emerged. It became more mainstream by the mid-1990s, allowing individuals to communicate easily across the room or around the world. It changed our culture and opened up widespread communication.

Okay, I don't want to bore you with history, but I'm amazed how history has changed communications and communications has changed history. This quick compression of history from Creation to present day teaches us several lessons.

One communication method doesn't make another obsolete.

The audience is the same but different. Ultimately, the medium has a certain *audience* potential and limitations. We need to use the methods as effectively as possible to communicate effectively.

The content needs to change with each method.

Each medium has certain *messaging* potential and limitations. Sometimes, the message determines the method with which it should be delivered while, many times, the method shapes the message.

The local church needs to use the best tools available.

Our message doesn't change, but the method needs to change based on the comfort level of our audience. The church bulletin isn't the "wrong way" to communicate, but perhaps, there's a "better way" to communicate to your audience. We, as church communicators, shouldn't be so concerned about maintaining "how we've always done it" but more about understanding how we can use the latest accepted way of communicating. We were born to communicate!

For Such a Time as This

Imagine. We aren't restricted to word-of-mouth, handwritten messages, newspapers, television, or print material. Instead, God put us on Earth at a time when you, practically alone, can influence the world for what you're known for. What a crazy time! You can tweet a message and have it instantly transmitted around the world and discovered by millions who engage with Twitter. What an opportunity! But what a burden.

God wants us to use the tools we've been given effectively to reach this world for Him. The best way to do that? Be known for something so that your community, your greater region, and the world will be attracted to you and you can influence them for Jesus Christ.

How can we do that? Why does the local church struggle with transitioning from print materials to other more effective communication methods? Bulletins and worship guides continue to abound when so much is stacked against them.

Print is (almost) dead.

Yet, it's still the lifeblood of most church communications. The world around us is slowly drifting away from printed materials. So, perhaps, the local church needs to consider a better way. When trends show that people prefer another method, the local church needs to take notice. Most newspapers and magazines are reducing their page counts as subscriptions continue to drop. You're probably one of the millions who haven't picked up a newspaper in years. The last recession accelerated this decline as the internet offers a more cost-effective method of delivering news and distributing advertising. Coupled with the acceleration of mobile devices where instant news alerts and free information abounds, print is dying. Why does the local church hang on? Local church leaders are scared of the potential resistance that might occur if, for example, they got rid of the weekly bulletin or worship guide.

Your audience is aging.

Most churches are aging upward. Studies are showing that the Millennials (the largest demographic group in America) are leaving the local church faster than any other generation. This skews our congregation's age higher than the community's. So, because most people attending church regularly are older, many of the members who haven't fully adopted digital are insisting that their bulletin stay intact. They trust it.

Content

For the most part, the content isn't the issue for the dying bulletin. People need the information it contains, and people want to find it easily. But people have to keep print materials just in case they ever need the information while new media delivers just-in-time information. When someone wants the content, they simply go to a URL to get it. It's never lost if your website is managed correctly.

Over the years, I have watched the transition in our own studio. Most of our designers stopped referring to the print magazines that I'd been collecting for inspiration. During one of our team meetings, I asked them if anyone had referred to printed magazines in the last six months. Not one. We instantly stopped all subscriptions. My studio schooled me that brainstorming could be accomplished easier online.

People want the news, but they want it instantly when they want it. And they only want exactly what they need.

So why does the bulletin demand still exist? The older the audience, the more they rely on print. But even for those who rely on the internet in their day-to-day dealings, many still want the church bulletin. Here's a possible reason…

The Church Bulletin Nazi

Almost every church in recent history has had a flyer, a bulletin, or a worship guide. But more importantly, there's usually one staff person assigned to oversee the content process. That person has grown so attached to this project that he or she takes it very personally. Everything must be delivered to this person by a specific time, on a specific day, and in a specific manner. If anything doesn't get delivered properly, you will not get your information in *her* (based on my experience, most of these people are women) bulletin! After all, *everything* has been proofed already. Because the Church Bulletin Nazi has experienced the wringer for errors in the past, she will die before anything ever appears inaccurate in *her* bulletin. The material is correct.

The Problem

Most of the world is drifting toward finding information online. Even the trusted church bulletin doesn't get read because we decide to find information on the church website. And the Church Bulletin Nazi's process breaks down. People either can't find the information, or they discover that the information is incorrect.

Delivering real-time information requires real-accurate information that's easily available. Unfortunately, many in our churches have realized it's easier to return to the prized and trusted publication called the bulletin. It's pushed to them by the ushers every Sunday, and they keep it as a Bible bookmark just in case they ever need to refer to it throughout the week. But they seldom do because people aren't motivated to scan through print materials anymore.

It's a crazy cycle we need to break.

Discussion #14

Do we communicate well to our congregation?

Do we communicate well to our community?

What tools do we use well?

What tools should we learn to use better?

Name our bulletin nazi. What do you think he/she thinks about change? About moving to another tool priority (other than print)?

Do people in our congregation actually read the bulletin? How can we find out?

Want additional information, downloads, and worksheets? Join us at www.beknownbook.com.

15

YOU NEED A COMMUNICATION STRATEGY

By now, you know that being known for something requires control and early decisions for certain things so that a benefit can be communicated consistently, emotionally, visually, and regularly.

But all of this effort will be wasted if you don't touch your audience with your visual brand and brand promise the way they want it. That's why you need to develop a strategy. If you don't have a communications strategy, you'll overspend and waste time.

Have you ever been sitting with a friend and sharing a problem you had? With great delight, your friend tells you about a product they've purchased that can solve your problem. You immediately Google it, only to find it's not available anymore. If the problem you're having isn't rare, this means that the solution's manufacturer hasn't communicated it well enough to prevent its demise.

This sounds so simple, but churches are closing every day because we're not effectively communicating to attract people who need what we have to offer.

The first part of this book dealt with determining how to voice your solution. Now, here are the steps to communicating it properly.

Having instructed and worked with hundreds of churches, I believe this is the simplest way to set up church communications that keeps your congregation happy while becoming a light to your community. Both audiences *need* to hear your thread.

Here are the seven steps to creating your strategy to reach the people who need a relationship with Jesus.

1: Define your thread.

Understand, support, and promote your be-known-for-something concept: the benefits, solutions, and paths to goals that are promised as part of your church's brand story. Wear your "thread glasses" 100% of the time. These imaginary glasses will enable you to see every ministry component, church area, and internal/external communication through the lens of your brand with the goal of aligning even the smallest elements with your thread. This can be done verbally, concept-wise, and visually. For example, if your thread is about "finding joy," the word "happy" would get shifted to "joy" in your church communications. Or, in creating a Christmas card design, "Joy to the World" would become a logical theme. If your branding uses PMS 185 Red, then every red in every area of your church needs to be as close to Pantone 185 as possible.

Without going absolutely crazy and overly cliché, your glasses will enable you to weigh everything against your thread benefit. To be known for something, you must marry as many things to your thread as possible. We'll discuss this more in Chapter 22.

2: Establish a visual brand with a clear graphic standard.

The rules of your graphic standard need to be written down, communicated, and understood by anyone creating any communication material on behalf of your church.

You'll also need an effective means to approve every communication piece with a process to revise anything that breaches the brand foundations. This approval process can be centralized (preferably) or decentralized, but everyone must be working with the same brand foundation document. No rogue ministries breaking the boundaries without consent of everyone.

At the same time, there does need to be an allowance for changing components of the graphic standard; however, this rare occurrence needs to be communicated to everyone but only after careful consideration of the impact to your brand.

3: Ensure your ministry's leadership is on board.

In order to be truly known for your brand, you must have authority granted by the senior leadership of the church. This authority is to encourage all ministries, as you empower without restricting the outreach of the church. There must be a mutual respect between the communications team and the senior leadership who always has veto powers. That's why it's essential to have the leadership's support and approval of each component of this strategy.

Successful churches don't have ministry silos because every ministry leader should be working toward establishing the main thread and brand of the church. The communications team subordinately works with leadership toward that goal.

4: Establish tiered communications.

In most churches, a message will be the most widely heard and understood in this order (based on where it's delivered or received):

- From the preacher in the pulpit
- From the pulpit during the announcement time
- In the pre-service video (unless it's too long)
- In a short email e-blast
- The rotating banner on your website
- Other areas of your website
- Posters in the church
- In the traditional printed newsletter
- In the bulletin/worship guide

Therefore, the most valuable advertising location is the preacher in the pulpit! So, of course, everyone wants their important announcement to happen there. Can you imagine if everyone got their way? We'd have a service of announcements with a song or two and only time for one verse of Scripture. And your congregation would flee your services.

There's a better way, a tiered communication mechanism in which you determine how important an announcement is in order to decide where (and how) it can be promoted.

Here are three tiers that will work for most churches (with an optional fourth):

First Tier

Imagine the layers of a multi-layered cake, and this is the large base. It's the largest foundational real estate. If a ministry event will interest at least 85% of the congregation, the event is firmly first-tier. A sermon series, an all-church meeting, or a community serving day would qualify as almost everyone is invited.

Second Tier

The second tier is similar to the first tier except that qualifying ministry events are trying to reach more than 85% of that specific ministry's population, so it could be viewed as that specific ministry's "tier one." These are their biggest events. Examples would include student ministry meetings, children's church gatherings, deaf ministry year-end celebration, etc.

Third Tier

This tier is for any other ministry event that's reaching less than 85% of a ministry, including things like small group meetings, teacher meetings, parking attendant meetings, etc.

Fourth Tier (optional)

This tier is reserved for outside groups that may be using your church for their events such as a Christian rock concert, Alcoholics Anonymous, denominational meetings, etc.

This isn't rocket science or anything original. You can start with this tier structure and adapt it for your needs. Perhaps, you may need to add another tier or remove one. The point is to prioritize ministry events in order to structure your strategy around them. What does this accomplish? It communicates that all events are not created equal, yet all are valuable and important.

Please note that, when an event is closely connected to your thread—the thread solution, the thread benefit, and the thread path—that event *can* move up to the next tier. Through its existence and communication, it will help to emphasize what the church is known for.

A really cool benefit of letting your staff know this? They'll creatively ensure their events become part of what the entire church is known for.

If you discover you have too many ministry events that qualify for first tier, edit the list by determining which of these "thread" announcements are intended for the greatest amount of people who will hear it.

5: Have one, easy-to-access event communication calendar.

Whether it's a digitally accessed calendar, an actual printed calendar, or a large wrap-around-the-room calendar on whiteboards, you need a centralized place for all events to be scheduled. The easiest way to do this is to have a regular communications meeting with all ministry staff considering an event. The sole purpose of the meeting is to discuss the communications calendar and planning for the year. Remember that this is a complete listing of all ministry events prior to them being announced anywhere. As you'll see, it doesn't make sense to have random smaller meetings to add events. It's wise to have any additions, changes, or deletions handled by the communications staff and, possibly, one person to eliminate errors.

Because your church is a subset of your community, be sure to check with the schools and the city regularly for all large "non-church" events that may affect your congregation. Add them to the calendar first (they can be color-coded if you'd prefer). Then, add tier one events, tier two events, tier three events, and then tier four events... in a cascading structure. You can color-code for tiers and/or ministries to help identify types of events if you'd prefer.

To have something added to the calendar, the ministry does not have to have all the details. It's likely that only the date, the idea, and who's invited will be needed. Though, the remaining details must be supplied later as part of the Transactional Communication Strategy (see below).

The communications team needs to advocate for your families during this process. Regularly scan the calendar to see how much stress a family would experience to participate as an active member. Then, consider facilities management, room allocation, and any other church issues that could affect your calendar such as snow removal, parking, weather, etc.

6: Keep it friendly.

You may have to ask a ministry to move an event due to an overlap or too many adjacent events. Tier one events get date preference over everything except community events. Then, tier two. Then, tier three. Then, tier four. Because tier four events rarely have date flexibility, you may have to refuse the outside group or voluntarily change internal tiered events to make the change.

Only after something remains on the calendar at the end of the meeting can a ministry externally communicate the date.

7: List all available communication tools.

As a communications team, you need a complete list of every possible communication tool available regularly for promoting a church event that's listed on the communications calendar. Some may be controlled by the ministry but approved by the communication team, and most will be produced and controlled by your team. Note any outside costs that are required.

Once you have the complete list, you'll need to decide the timeframe that it will take to design, proof, get approvals, and produce/post material for that tool. Consider the regular workload and amount of staff you have on your team when deciding these timeframes. I would suggest adding some buffer time into each one (e.g. three weeks for website home banner, four weeks for lobby banner stand, two weeks for social media ad, etc.).

Transactional Communication Strategy

One of the biggest concerns I hear from church leadership is that the communications staff say "no" quickly, and it's difficult to get materials in a timely fashion. This strategy changes that.

Think about it like shopping. Every ministry (based on tiering) has the ability to "purchase" communications... not with money (other than production, programming, and/or printing costs needed) but with this transactional strategy (tier, tools, and time).

Here are the rules...

First-Tier Events

Their organizers should get everything they would like from the tool list, or you can give them a certain quantity of items from which they can choose. However, there are certain tools available only for the top tier. For example, only first tier events would qualify for pulpit announcements, video announcements, the main rotating web banner, a top-level mention in your e-blast, etc. They can get other communication tools, too, based on how you want to set this up.

Plus, they *must* have the ability to supply materials to you based on the requirements for using the tool. Something can go on the calendar without all the details, but the timeframe for "purchasing" the communication tool must be met, or the tool will not be available to them.

Second-Tier Events

Fewer tool options will be available for these than for first tier events. For example, they may get bulletin space (with a limited amount of words and content), a secondary area on the home page, a graphic on their specific ministry's page, a calendar listing, and a banner in the ministry area. Remember that you should create this list for what will work in *your* church!

Plus, they *must* have the ability to supply materials to you based on the requirements for using the tool. Something can go on the calendar without all the details, but the timeframe for "purchasing" the communication tool must be met, or the tool will not be available to them.

Third-Tier Events

As a reminder, these events don't tie directly to your thread and don't speak to a large audience. Ultimately, it may be better to personally email the eight people interested in it. The organizers still need the ability to promote their event but with far fewer tools. They may only get a website calendar listing and something that the leaders will send out (email) or handout.

Plus, they *must* have the ability to supply materials to you based on the requirements for using the tool. Something can go on the calendar without all the details, but the timeframe for "purchasing" the communication tool must be met or the tool will not be available to them.

Once something is on the calendar and the tools have been selected, set up timeframe reminders for materials. You may need to notify ministry leaders before material deadlines. This is entirely up to your church and can possibly be automated on a digital calendar.

This strategy helps logistically with managing ministries, time, and tools. Be sure that everyone understands and agrees to each component so there are no surprises! Note that it's essential for the senior leadership to agree not to create exceptions to this. We realize that "someone" will know "Rev. Leader" who wants to bypass the system and initialize a precedence. We know it will happen; however, it needs to be navigated carefully. Afterward, simply reset and start fresh with using the system again.

Pray that no one noticed the knitting club main stage announcement that the senior pastor's wife leads. Leadership approval is key although we know that politics in the church can mess with the strategy.

Important Note

Remember that part of the "purchasing agreement" for all tiers is to have the approved event added to a centralized communication calendar, allowing enough planning and production time to accomplish the tier (predetermined by you and communicated fairly and equally to every ministry). All accurate materials should be delivered to you when required based upon a certain amount of creative and production time before the event (again predetermined and communicated fairly). Also, there must be an agreement to assess the outcomes after the event with their leadership and the communication leadership.

Thread Magic

From the moment we're born, we want more than we deserve. The same happens when you roll out this system. What we observe is that ministry leaders often don't like not being able to get what they don't qualify for (because of the tier they're in).

This is where *thread magic* can happen. Here's how it works.

When a ministry wants additional communication tools or treatment that their tier doesn't qualify them for, there's a solution! Simply ask them to align their specific event or promotion creatively with your church thread.

If they do that, you'll consider...

- Moving their event up one tier-level, granting to them all the communication rights and privileges of the new tier.

- And/or, you may grant to them an additional amount of communication rights and privileges. That's entirely at your discretion (e.g. access to two additional communication tools). You pre-determine this fairly for all, based on your work-load and the ability to provide the additional materials.

What does this "thread magic" produce?

- Alleviates the unrest of saying they can't have something. You don't have to just say no!
- Allows them to support the overall church thread, which helps reduce ministry silos within you church and builds your church brand.
- Reinforces your church thread, stimulating crea-tivity within various ministries.

Additional community communication questions to consider (and additional external communication tools)

Where are your personas located?

You can reach your congregation as they arrive at your campus or engage with your communication tools. But for your commu-nity (people who don't fully know your church), this gets extremely difficult. Consider where your personas live, hangout, and dwell. Look for similarities. Do they regularly gather at the same location? Is there something about their demographics or psychographics that would suggest their location? You know they're also online, but where online? Probably social media, YouTube, Netflix, and other regular online hangouts... but what about more obscure locations? What about finding them in the things they read? AutoTrader? Apartment Magazines? It's important to know where people are so you can communicate to them.

Are they reachable there?

Once located, start thinking about how you can talk to your personas there. You can call them, send direct mail to them, put ads in places they'll discover, etc. Also, think about every possible communication device that's available, and consider adding them to the list of tools you offer (with a timeframe and price associated with them).

What's your budget?

This often will help with making decisions. Remember that limitations are often the foundation of creativity and invention. Consider how much money you (or the individual ministries) have or how much money a person is "worth" to share your message with them. Consider how to reach as many as possible at once to help lower the cost.

Limited budget? Consider co-op advertising (where you share the expense with others who want to reach the same audience), volunteer communicators, and other existing opportunities. Often, if churches simply used all the opportunities it already has correctly (like signs, announcements, mailers, social media, website, etc.), they could reach their communities for Christ.

Frequency

As my kids were growing up, my wife and I wanted to get them to respond right away when we requested something. Our mantra was "delayed obedience is disobedience." We did everything possible to get an instant response. And, we often failed. Most of the world don't attempt to train their kids that way. So, people aren't geared to respond immediately when they hear a message once. That's why it's imperative that you create campaigns. These are assembled, controlled, and consistent groups of communications designed to say your message over and over... until they listen.

How many times will you have to post, purchase, say, write, etc.? Who knows? In all my decades of monitoring this, it's more than you'd suspect.

A trick that secular industry does? They repeat it in short bursts, take a breather, and do another short burst. Often on TV (if it's an annual campaign), it's 13 weeks on... 13 weeks off... 13 weeks on... 13 weeks off. People are tricked into believing that it's on all the time, but it only costs half as much as running an ad continuously. Ultimately, it's difficult to over-saturate your community with a message, especially on most church budgets. The main point? You must say it more than once... maybe, twice or more. You need to figure out how many times it is.

Message

This is the content of what you're promoting. In order to develop a strong brand, you need to have pure branding campaigns. This isn't to promote any particular product of the church. It's actually advertising the benefit of your church, your thread.

The local church needs to stop being seen as product promoters so we can start being known for something much bigger than our products. So, have a brand thread—which is... say it with me now... what you want to be known for—and then have products or services that you want people to adopt.

Your message should *always* point to your thread benefit. If it doesn't, I wouldn't promote it to your community widespread. Instead, directly communicate it to your smaller group if at all.

Discussion #15

Do we have a clear, written graphic standard that describes the parameters of our brand?

Is our leadership totally on-board with our brand and thread?

Are all of our ministries aware of what tier they're on and why? Are we?

Are the ministries aware of what tools are at their disposal, based on their tier?

Are they aware of how they can have more communications if they tie their event to the thread? What more can you offer when they use "thread magic"?

Is our leadership aware that they can't change the rules or make exceptions on a regular basis? Do they know what will occur if they do?

Want additional information, downloads, and worksheets? Join us at www.beknownbook.com.

16

WORD-OF-MOUTH PROMOTION

Communications can be costly as you try to connect your message to your audience. Inevitably, churches suggest they rely on word-of-mouth promotions. Usually, this is because they perceive it as costing nothing to do. As I suggested earlier in this book, this is a highly effective promotion tool, but it takes time... lots of time.

Word-of-mouth promotion is another ambitious way of saying you want something to go "viral." Most people view this as...

> Our church wants something totally free that somehow will make everyone share it with everyone they meet. Then, those people will pass it on to everyone they know so that, soon, everyone will know about it. And ultimately, we won't have to pay for any marketing or communications.

Wouldn't that be wonderful! But, it's impossible.

Occasionally, of course, everything in a campaign aligns, and the timing is perfect so that a message takes off with greater success than expected. I like to call it the God-factor because the joy of working with the local church is that God often miraculously steps in and accelerates the outcome greater than we'd ever imagine. It's one of the main reasons why I love working with the local church!

While working with one church a few years ago, we created an Easter promotion. The children's pastor, who I was privileged to work with, taught me so much about creating viral buzz. He was a talented communicator and loved to dream big. Often, he would chide me and challenge me to think much bigger than my comfort level.

This church wanted something that would attract kids from the city that the church was in. They did a huge Christmas outreach, but Easter had always been a challenge. He proposed doing an Easter egg hunt and asked if we could help him dream big with it. After several possibilities were presented, the idea of doing the "World's Largest Easter Egg Hunt" was suggested. A little research indicated it would take a lot of eggs. Interestingly, the idea of breaking a world record for a wholesome family event led to a call being received from a large chocolate company. Within days, the church got approval for a donation of 250,000 solid chocolate Easter eggs.

Within the church, information spread immediately, and the word-of-mouth promotion got big. The church started getting calls, and interest spread. We realized the church building was not big enough to hide a quarter-million Easter eggs. A local park was even too small. We realized it had to be even bigger. Finally, the city's promotional department was engaged. After much conversation, planning, and assistance, the hunt became regional. On the day of the hunt, the city shut down the entire downtown core in order to let the church hide their eggs. The media was notified, and the entire region started talking about the "huge" Easter egg hunt.

The church ended up not having to pay very much to promote it at all. The idea became viral, and this was before social media was even a term.

That event enabled the church to provide an Easter egg bag with the Easter story (and how it can change their lives) printed on the side for almost 10,000 kids. The city placed a stage for the church in front of city hall and allowed the children's department to present songs, drama, and the message of the gospel. The story of the Easter egg hunt made it to the front page of the newspaper the following day!

Before you try to emulate this event, may I warn you that this event started my need to be concerned about details before, during, and after the event. Here are some details that we wished we had considered.

First, kids who hear "quarter of a million" solid chocolate Easter eggs hear "I'm going to find a *ton* of Easter eggs." Kids and adults showed up with large garbage bags to stash their loot while other smaller children used our small collection bags to roam the downtown core and find eggs as a fun family event. If you divide 250,000 by 10,000 kids, you get 25 eggs each... if they got distributed equally.

Second, when you produce an Easter event in the North, you need to anticipate cold weather, especially when it's an outdoor event. No one anticipated the freak snowstorm that blessed us with 10 inches of fluffy snow over the hunt area. The best thing? It kept our crowd down to "only" 10,000 people. The problem, though? It created a cold, wet environment but allowed us to hide the eggs easily as we simply dropped the foil-covered eggs so they disappeared into the snow.

Third, if you're trying to break a world record officially, you must involve *The Guinness Book of World Records*. And they have rules. And rules. And rules. The biggest one for us? In order for it to be a "hunt," *all* eggs must be hidden from view and not simply "clumped" together. The snow helped with this, but it was difficult to hide them in foyers, reception areas, and theaters. Simply put, it was hard to hide that many eggs.

We had a large group of about 100 people who volunteered to hide the eggs. The hunt was planned for a morning, so the church met with the volunteers before daybreak to give directions for hiding the eggs and have a time of prayer. We thought we had plenty of time. Every person was tasked to hide about 2,500 eggs. The city allowed us about an hour of access to the downtown before the event as they were concerned about putting eggs out too early in such a large area. Each person, including me as a volunteer, ended up having to hide about 41 eggs *every* minute for an hour.

Trying to hide an egg completely every second and a half without clustering them proved impossible. And for this reason, the onsite Guinness representative disqualified the event because some volunteers thought it would be easier to roll eggs under the seats of the downtown theater where they pooled at the bottom and weren't hidden when the kids entered.

Lastly, when 10,000 people run through a downtown area in a frantic search, the big people win, and the little ones don't. A church can't tell people to collect only 25 eggs each. So, a positive outcome didn't happen. In less than 20 minutes, the eggs were all gone... along with every snow bank in the city core. Many adults had large, full bags of eggs and, sadly, many young children (accompanied by very angry parents) were seen crying with tears running into their empty bags. The next day, the newspaper dedicated a large portion of their front page to a picture of a man grinning from ear to ear while toting a large bag of Easter eggs and passing a crying, distraught child. The headline? Something like, "Is our city known for greed?"

Lessons Learned

Plan every event as though it will go viral, and ensure your plans anticipate worst-case scenarios. Huge viral events are not always the best, so be careful what you pray for!

Over my years of studying social media, the internet, and talking to those who've had viral hits, I've learned five criteria about creating an event worthy of amazing word-of-mouth promotion.

1: Your idea needs to be shocking, surprising, unique, and worthy of general participation.

This is a tall order. I'm amazed by how many videos and ideas still go viral. I think it comes from a human's desire for spectating and enjoying good entertainment.

2: It usually requires people to know a brand association so they will quickly buy into the event.

It helped that our Easter egg hunt had the city's name attached and that the church had high awareness because of their large Christmas outreach. Remember that, to have a brand, you need to be known for something in your community (personas). Hopefully, it's positive!

3: You need a simple, unexpected benefit.

Word of mouth requires a key benefit that's simple, easily remembered, and quickly reiterated. People also love to tell stories with unexpected endings... like a good joke that makes someone feel good. It must be remembered, the right reaction must be anticipated, and the person must feel rewarded for telling it. Many announcements in a church are too complex, having many details that don't have to do with the simple benefit of participating.

4: You need a "tipping point."

Connect to the right people who will ignite the word-of-mouth discussions, or you must place an ad or post in the right location so it will take off. This is easier said than done. Instead, I would start a paid promotional plan to push the message and then reduce it when it becomes viral. Remember that very few events, videos, or posts become viral!

5: You need validation.

To capture attention through word of mouth, there has to be a professional, believable website with all the details plus justification of the unbelievable benefit to participating in your event.

A website should be the core of all your communications. It allows those "talking" about you simply to remember a URL so they don't have to remember the details. Or, it must be Google-able, which requires good search engine optimization.

You probably don't always want something to "take off" with a life of its own. If you just want positive buzz about your church, you simply want to be known for something that is a benefit to the people hearing it, which is exactly what this book has shown you how to do.

Someone described *luck* as simply being ready when an unusual alignment of circumstances occurs that benefits you. It's being in the right place at the right time and fully ready. That's really what word of mouth requires. It's about determining what you're known for, having the communication processes in place, and having God show up to give you an amazing opportunity that He's prepared you for.

If your message requires much more than 30 seconds to share, it's too complex. Keep it very simple!

Imagine what it was like at the turn of the 20th century. You had a message to deliver with an amazing benefit for your audience, but you had limited options for getting that message out.

You had to stand in front of your business or organization and shout it out or hand out flyers. People who had more money could get an ad in the newspaper or on the radio. Now, we have so many more options to allow a message to find its way to an audience!

We just need to have a director who can control the process and message.

Discussion #16

What are our thoughts about word-of-mouth promotion? Is it possible at our church? With our leaders?

What specific ministry in our church has the potential to "go viral" with one of their events?

How can we encourage it? Is it worth it?

Want additional information, downloads, and worksheets? Join us at www.beknownbook.com.

17

COMMUNICATION DIRECTOR

To build a solid, trusted digital hub for your church, you will need a director, someone who will be a possessive, process-driven owner of your entire communications with the website, which is central to your digital hub. This can be a director of communication, a communication coordinator, a secretary in charge of communication, or a talented volunteer with communication on his or her mind.

Here's what makes a good church communicator:

Understands the creative process and likes to build teams

Most bulletin *Nazis* operate in silos, either because they've driven everyone crazy or because they haven't been given the budget to utilize anyone else. Not so for an effective church communicator. Instead, you're looking for someone who is creative, resourceful, team-oriented, and inspiring. "We're all in this together, so let's figure out a great solution that we haven't thought of before" should be this person's motto.

Loves the work of ministry

Should I have to write this? This key person must enjoy the work-ings of the local church, your church, and have the desire to use his or her talents to help people be transformed by the gospel message. If your communications director ever loses sight of this, you're in trouble. You'll simply have a tyrant in charge of a criti-cal process and who very few like. They'll get their work done but at what cost? Ministry-hearted people put others first and help to support, encourage, and motivate the great work going on around your church.

Attention to details and process

This is a very important part of a church communicator's job; however, most creatives are not drawn to details. Usually, you either will have a creative or a detail-oriented person. Because of this, you should form a creative team so the shortcomings of the lead creative (who is the rarer find) can be supported by a detail-oriented assistant.

Everyone needs a communication process... much like the locked-down bulletin process. Other ministry leaders in your church must know the rules of the process and agree to follow them. If the process changes too many times, it's not a process; it's called chaos. This is the problem you're trying to solve rather than create. Rather than managing people, manage the commu-nication process while asking people to follow it in a loving way.

Loves to edit

Simplicity is the key to good communications. A church *must* have a good editor in order to create effective engagement. If you're not editing, you're over-communicating, which discon-nects you from your audience. Everyone wants real-time information delivered in bite-sized chunks. People don't like long paragraphs, so they simply scan material instead of reading. If it's taking too long, your audience has stopped reading.

Our churches don't need more content. They need edited content. Less. Eliminate fluff, and deliver bullet points, tweet-capable (140 characters or less) content that allows eye interruptions to catch attention.

Is worthy of church leadership

This position needs to be part of the key leadership of the church and have a seat at the decision table. The position may not be at the executive level (although it should be), but the person in the role must be worthy of senior leadership. This person should be capable of understanding why core ministry decisions are being made and allowed to help make decisions because they're advocating for your congregation and community. If your communications person doesn't have the power to say "no" within the church leadership, you're crippling the process and weakening the power of great church communications.

It makes sense for this person to be a full-time staff person for medium-sized and large churches because communicating everything effectively takes a lot of time. However, for smaller churches, the role can be spread over several people or clearly added to the job description of a secretary or assistant.

If you can't afford to hire someone, consider tasking someone with creating a volunteer group that consists of people who understand the challenge. Someone will need to motivate, create expectations, and set deadlines for them. This person needs to work as a liaison between executive leadership and the volunteer group. He or she must understand the direction of ministry and give suggestions and feedback to the pastors.

Skills can be taught and acquired. Your church needs a talented team who can plan, create a process, conceptualize, write and edit, take photographs, design (Adobe Creative Suite skills for Illustrator and Photoshop, etc.), shoot video, do post-production editing (After Effects skills, etc.), and have website development, programming, content management, and presentation skills.

This is why it's difficult to find one person who has all of these skills and why most churches can't afford a team that can do them either. Nor should you! Most of the skills aren't needed on a regular basis, so it's better to use freelancers, volunteers, or a creative/design agency who's available on a retainer.

Or, do what you can based on your current skills, slowly adding people to the team as you can. Just be careful that you don't add unnecessary complexity and expectations to the process that you can't maintain because of skills or time.

The one task most communication directors don't do.

In this role, it's one thing to set goals, motivate great communication work, and supply creative materials to all the ministries in your church. But the one task most don't do? They don't do the necessary meetings for follow-up, debriefing, or encouragement. Your job is not done until you've assessed what's been done, checked if goals have been accomplished, and noted how to improve in the future. This shouldn't be a negative meeting; it should be encouraging, motivating, and short.

Discussion #17

Does our church need a full-time communication director?

Could someone do it part-time? Who?

The person doing that position now… is he/she sitting at the leadership table? If not, how can we get him/her there?

Want additional information, downloads, and worksheets? Join us at www.beknownbook.com.

18

PRINT HUB TO DIGITAL HUB CONVERSION

With the right people, you can make the conversion from a print-centric hub to a digital-centric hub. As with people throughout history who have had to switch from doing verbal communications to finding the benefits of using print communications, you'll find the transformation will be difficult, but you'll enjoy so many of its benefits! Here are four simple steps:

1: Create a simple website structure to make it easy for people to find content.

Remember this is not *your* information; it's *their* information that's needed. Don't get territorial with your content. Instead, it must be created and organized for the people who will consume it. The sitemap (the hierarchical chart of all content on a website) must be formulated from *their* vantage point. They must find the information that's needed regularly near the top of the website (as close to your homepage as possible). Websites are structured around menus that must answer obvious questions based on what you're known for.

You want to be known for joyful living? The main menu selections could focus on leading people to answers to the question of how to experience joyful living. The phrase on the website could be "How you do that."

Drop-down menus should contain the information people are looking for under the main menu. If most people aren't looking for that information, remove the menu listing and consider what main page should have a link to the less-important information. Analytics tracking such as Google Analytics can be added to any website to give you insight into who's reading your website. These analytics will help in this step. If no one is going to a page, there's a great reason to stop providing that information (or figuring out a cleverer way of delivering it).

Some churches have websites that nobody is visiting while others have website pages that no one is reading! That's a waste of time and money. Websites should attract people. If yours doesn't, you need to change it. Start with improving the organization of your website's content.

2: Create a friendly, simple user interface (UI) that employs a strategy so people can find, read, and share information without the design getting in the way (UX).

There are many studies that track eye movements when people go to a webpage. It helps us to understand what most expect when they go to websites. That's called the *web paradigm*.

I travel all over North America and stay in various hotels in random cities. When a hotel is kind enough to offer me a free newspaper (yes, the only kind of newspaper I read), I pick it up and recognize it as a newspaper. I know how to get around it and find the information I'm looking for. Newspapers don't all look exactly alike, but there's an underlying similarity that's been developed and approved over many decades. That's the newspaper paradigm.

Because it's only been a few years since websites have become commonplace, people are surprised that we even have a paradigm. So I hear from designers (and some leaders) that they want to create a different website so their church will have a "creative" website. That pretty much ensures they will have an unread website. If you break the web paradigm, people won't understand where things are, and things won't feel natural to them. It's better to aim for "regular" when it comes to interface, but be creative within the paradigm's fences.

That should make sense to you. Like picking up a newspaper that doesn't follow the paradigm, you'd need an instructional manual to figure everything out. It would take longer to get what you want. Many websites slow people down when the person's ultimate goal is to spend as little time as possible to find what they're looking for on your website.

Let's review website paradigm so you can understand things you shouldn't seek to alter. Remember, though, this paradigm may shift in the future. Websites are changing regularly, so these ideas are quite broad.

Current Web Paradigm

Upper-left corner

Almost everyone looks here in the header when going to a website. They're looking for a simple confirmation that they're at the correct website. They've input or clicked on a URL address, and now, they've arrived. Confirm that they're at the right place by putting your logo here. It can be small, but it should be there.

And because you've captured most people's attention (even for only a fraction of a second), what else should be in this high-priced real estate? Your be-known-for-something thread… as a simple tagline under the logo, perhaps.

Header

People look for a header area that runs to the right of the logo at the top of the page. They expect to see a menu to the bottom-right of the header. (Menus can also be down the left side of the page, but most are at the top.) A search area is often found in the upper-right side of the header along with a login area or "contact us" section. Churches often use this space for important information like service times, locations, and directions as most congregation and community members visiting the website would want this information regularly.

Main content area

This is where the content is delivered. It's typically in the center below the header. Because the average person spends 8-10 seconds on a page, they want this content to be what they expect… that is, scannable or browsed in a *very* short time. Approximately 50 words is all that an average American can read in that timeframe (based on the 300-words-per-minute national average).

Remember that headlines are read first. Most people will only read the first few words of the headline because we're not reading everything, and we're scared of the right side of the page (keep reading).

Right side of the content area

Thanks to web paradigm, ads are usually found on the right side of the content area, so people tend to avoid that side to avoid getting tricked into clicking on something unexpected. Only 15-20% of people will ever look at content there. And because of this avoidance, people scan content and value the content on the left as more important than content on the right side.

Long pages with modules

Thanks to our migration to mobile devices (phone and tablet) to access our web content, websites need to be as easily viewed on a small screen as on a large desktop monitor. This seamless resizing is called *responsiveness*. On a mobile device, it's easier to swipe upward than to click on small links with your thumb, so the longer page with many modules is taking over web paradigm. Just remember to treat modules like you would pages. Keep the content short, and create eye interruptions in the design to indicate where to stop and start when scanning the page.

3: Create a content strategy.

It's critical to use your communication tools properly. Having a tool doesn't make you use it the best way. Like many people, I have a BBQ grill, but I can't say I use it properly. Recently, a friend grilled for us, serving an amazing meal cooked over the hot coals on his outdoor grill. It doesn't matter if you have the right grill equipment; it's the way things are cooked on it, the practice of getting it just right, and the quality of the ingredients that matter. That's what communication strategy is all about.

You can have the right tools (e.g. website, social media, bulletin, posters, etc.), but it's critical to use them properly based on feedback and to get the right content within them that determines the fine communications that you serve. These things will determine whether anyone enjoys the "meal."

It's incredibly important that your strategy continue changing incrementally. Create a process to establish your strategy in writing, including SMART goals (specific, measurable, achievable, relevant, and timed). Remember that goals that are written down usually generate better results. Why? Writing something down will enable you to decide on something specific and have it for accountability.

Write down what you want to communicate through the digital tools that are readily available to you. *Then*, incorporate print and verbal assistance as needed.

There are five steps to create a basic, functional strategy:

1. List every possible method or tool you'd like to use.
2. List your personas that represent your congregation and community.
3. Decide if you'll use some or all tools to reach each persona. Or, will a tool only reach one? You determine that. You may decide to drop a tool if you're not using it effectively, or you may commit to using it better.
4. Decide what your audience's concerns, needs, and pains are and how you'll address them. This is your be-known-for-something thread. Decide how the statement is interpreted by each audience and tool. For example, Instagram would require a picture, blogs would need great writing, and YouTube obviously needs video. Be specific!
5. Set a schedule, a ROI goal (return on investment), and desired outcome for all of your labor. This will be easier if you do it by audience or by method. Set a follow-up timeframe or mechanism that will hold you accountable. The more you're held accountable—first, by writing it down; then, by sharing it—the better your outcome will be.

Once you start this cycle of dreaming, writing, doing, and checking, you'll start realizing your successes and your failures. Checking requires excellent analytics, so ensure you have Google Analytics (or something similar) in place.

Probably the single biggest benefit of digital communications is that you can track successes and failures so much better than with any print material.

Realize you can't do everything well, though. In fact, say it aloud right now: "I can't do everything well." *Hey, why did you choose not to say it for all to hear?* You're scared that those near you will nod in agreement. So, stop acting like you can.

Instead of feeling like a failure, use your failures to decide who's needed on your team or how to do something differently within your comfort zone. Or (this is a huge one), maybe, you don't have to do it at all. However, if the outcome can't be reached and is still desired, you'll have to figure out a course-correction to achieve the goals.

I'm a goal-oriented person (my DiSC personality profile actually confirms this), so I *love* this step. Others of you (I'm looking at you, Ms. Creative and Mr. Designer) will find this to be a chore that is equivalent to going to the dentist regularly. Please understand… Don't go overboard with this process. Do it to the extent you feel comfortable.

Here's an example of how easy it can be.

I'm going to post blog articles from guest bloggers on our websites, short articles of 250-400 words each, about "finding joy in unexpected places" every week on Tuesdays at 3pm. Then, I'll post about the latest blog Wednesday mornings at 7:30 a.m. on LinkedIn and Facebook to reach business people, ages 30-50, before they head to work. I will aim to get one or two comments about each article. Between my LinkedIn and Facebook accounts, I currently have 300 followers in that demographic. I want to reach 400 within six months. I'll use Facebook ads ($25 per month) to attract more in that demographic by pushing people to the blog on the website.

It's that simple. All it requires? Dreaming about your end goal, using what you have, and following up. You will never be able to track success unless you write the goals down. Robert Collier said, "Success is the sum of small efforts repeated day in and day out."

Either start with goals you want to achieve and break down the tasks, or start with the people you want to reach and set goals. Then, create steps to accomplish those goals.

Being known for something starts with consistently communicating to the same audience the same positive benefit over and over again. Just start doing it!

4: Create a proofing paradigm.

Nothing can erode your communication strategy worse than having mistakes in your communications. Enlist your website or bulletin nazi to create a paradigm that insists on accuracy. I believe that the majority of people notice inaccuracies, typos, spelling errors, and other grammar mistakes and will instantly become skeptical of anything you say. When your audience starts to doubt you, that's the moment when they'll move on to find another trusted source. They'll revert to the old tried-and-true. When someone doubts the accuracy of a print communication piece, they'll start relying on the verbal announcement. If people doubt your website, they'll resist all of your digital activities and want to go back to the print materials they've trusted for a long time.

Let's have the local church set the standard of excellence in everything we're doing because we have the most important message that needs to be heard!

Discussion #18

Do we have too many print communications in our church?

Is there a reason?

Is our congregation ready to have our print communications go completely away? Be diminished?

Is our website ready to be the center of the digital hub?

What needs to be improved?

Does our congregation trust our content online? Is it easy to find and always up-to-date and correct?

What are the steps we need to take?

Want additional information, downloads, and worksheets? Join us at www.beknownbook.com.

19

OTHER DIGITAL COMMUNICATIONS

I've always enjoyed traveling and continue to drive great distances to see clients instead of opting for air travel. In Canada, there are signs on the divided multilane highways that say, "Keep right except to pass." It makes so much sense. I often find myself wanting to communicate that concept to people who are slowly driving in the left lane while a lineup of traffic is tailgating behind them. Finally, they get the hint and slowly make their lane change to let us proceed.

There's nothing worse than not being able to communicate when a message needs to be given.

I've always wished I had a programmable digital sign on my SUV that scrolls the messages I think. Don't get me wrong... I'm not a yeller or a gesturer. I've never understood people who get stressed inside their cars. If only they could have an outlet! Everyone wants to communicate and will try to do it as best as they can.

There are many means of communication (even without my vehicle signage idea). When I'm at the beach, my favorite place on earth, the planes stream long banners in the sky, advertising a restaurant or event. And people still leave gospel tracts on the urinals of men's rooms across America.

But just because there's a medium, that doesn't mean you should be using it. Did you hear that? You shouldn't use every method of communication just because you can or even because you can afford it.

That's why most people don't use TV, radio, or plane writing in the sky. The reasons to use a particular means of communication are that a large percentage of your audience is using it, reading it, or paying attention to it; your message is suited for it; and you can afford it.

Social media, web, and email are all being used more than print materials. Your audience is using these tools, so you should, too.

Here's the issue, though. These terms—social, web, and email—have become so generic that most people will say they're using these media. But now, there are so many options in each umbrella term, and you should *not* be using all of them.

This chapter risks being the first chapter that will require updating because so much is changing and growing, so I'll try to give more general direction and strategy.

Here are three concepts to guide you concerning these digital mediums.

1: Make sure your specific audience is regularly using it as you're intending.

Spending time or money to reach a small portion of your audience needs to be balanced with whether you're successful with everything else. I would dedicate time to where the majority of your audience is and ensure success there before you try to reach a fragment of your community. Facebook is the leader now and probably for a while, so if you're going to try social media, try

Facebook first and get it right before attempting the others. Almost everyone is on web and email, so these should also be part of your mix.

2: Make sure your product and thread is best suited for the delivery method.

Visual messages make sense on some tools. Because the majority of people respond first to video or image, I would try to develop a visual strategy for your message. But, maybe, your thread isn't necessarily visual. In that case, rule out those mediums and learn how to do words well (or create visual memes from your words).

3: Make sure you can afford it.

Look at the overall cost of registration, setup, updating, and responding. Consider not only the dollar cost but also the time cost. Your time is worth a lot more than most understand. And if you're using volunteers, consider their time valuable, too, because their time is limited. Your church should be good stewards of money and time. Costs should be weighed on the altar of goals. If you're not able to achieve your goals with the cost, your ROI (return on investment) is broken, and you need to consider doing something else. Period.

Here are some additional thoughts you should take into consideration regarding digital mediums. It's not exhaustive, but it is foundational thought.

Website Strategy

I'm sure you're thinking, "Well, duh... Of course, we have a website." And, yes, I believe every organization needs a web presence of some sort, even if it's a simple Facebook page. But consider all the other web possibilities. Everyone wants a successful website, but many don't have goals for their site.

Most churches have websites that are informative while the majority of people want to visit websites that are interactive and engaging. So, you need to push your web communications and seek to engage your church website visitors fully.

Ultimately, every website needs to have a strategy to funnel visitors onto a list.

The basic goal of your website should be to discover who is visiting your website and to keep a database of them so you can contact them via the website, phone, mail, or email... especially if they're interested in what you're known for! Your be-known-for-something thread is a benefit you'll need to share to grow a list of the people with the pain or solution you specialize in. They're potential followers and potential members of your congregation!

You're not selling to the list; your purpose is to help them. If the value of what you're offering is essential, they'll pay a high "cost." That's not necessarily money but something that requires time or effort. Costs can range from leaving an email or name on a form (the most basic) all the way to leaving a credit card attached to your website for regular, online giving. It could simply be subscribing to an online newsletter by filling out an informational form or taking a survey.

Remember that websites aren't just online brochures. They're online evangelists that operate like an expert help desk. And the best help desk employees listen more than they talk.

Unfortunately, many church websites simply talk. And talk. And talk. Instead, ask questions, get feedback, interact, share free resources, and enjoy the presence of people on your website. Try to offer enough value that, at minimum, people will leave their contact name and email address because they don't want to miss talking with you again!

Social Strategy

This is such a great way to engage with people in your congregation and your community. If you're operating it properly, it should be easy... almost second nature. Have fun getting to know who's following along!

I have several social media accounts that require a lot of effort to engage with the audience though. Except, I have one that I barely have to pay attention to. It's now my largest social audience with dozens joining weekly.

It's a Facebook page to gather people who suffer from *misophonia* (facebook.com/stopthesounds). A few years ago, I heard a brief mention of this affliction on the radio in which people are overly annoyed or debilitated because of certain sounds like hearing fingernails screeching on a blackboard. Except, misophonia goes beyond that reaction. Regular, repetitive sounds, including mouth and nose sounds, drive us crazy.

Yes, I'm part of this crazy community. Nose whistling, popping gum, mouth breathing, etc. will drive me to a place where I find it hard to function. I thought I was the only one who suffers from these triggers. I just figured I was crazy. In fact, I stopped asking people to stop the sounds. Thinking I was alone in my trigger world, I was excited to discover there actually was a name for it! I felt justified.

I searched Facebook for the term, misophonia, and at the time, there were no other pages (except for a band who adopted this strange name). Somewhat as a joke, I started the page and posted a brief self-deprecating post on my personal Facebook page. I was amazed. People started messaging me and admitting (like it was their deepest darkest sin) that they also suffer from it to varying degrees.

I posted a few times, and the page took off! At this writing, over 11,000 people have followed the page. I answer dozens of private messages monthly from people who feel ashamed to follow the page. People are seeking answers, help, and a listening ear. My mantra on the page is "We Understand."

I believe God is allowing me to use this page to minister and encourage people all around the world who would *never* connect with me in another way… especially on a religious level.

God is also allowing me to moderate the page so I can single-handedly watch the power of social media. I don't do most of the posting; the community does. They want to talk, interact, and get information from each other.

This should be your church's goal for social media.

Provide a place for engagement, interaction, and information. Stir the pot occasionally, but remain true to the purpose of your page. Keep offering your thread that they can't get anywhere else. A great social media page will have return visitors who desire what you're offering.

Think "entertain" rather than "inform" or "promote." Social media is likened to television when it comes to the amount of time people spend on it. As users, we treat it as a form of entertainment. When it stops being entertaining, we don't want to see it on our walls, so we hide or unfollow the page. Then, engagement is lost.

Let's learn from television. It has established a format that feels like 80% entertainment and 20% advertising. Rarely (except for maybe the Superbowl) will someone tune into a TV show for the advertising. We want the entertainment! Yet, on social media, churches and organizations promote and advertise themselves continuously. We think, "Because all of these people need to know what I'm known for, they'll listen to me!" But no one likes a person who sells constantly. Sadly, the average church page promotes their programs and events so much that one can only assume they care more about their programs than the people who come to the page.

Yes, promote yourself and what you're known for, but consider entertainment that your thread can ride on. And get really good at it. Entertain so well that they'll stay and listen to the promotion.

For example, if your thread is about experiencing genuine joy, showing short and unexpected videos of people experiencing joy together could demonstrate your value without pushing your next meeting. But people will be more apt to seek information about your meetings if they like who you are based on the majority of your entertaining posts.

Remember your audience and what you're known for.

As you're ultimately talking solutions, you'll also need to consider the pains, needs, and paths to goals and talk about them, too. You must become the expert on understanding what they're experiencing and solving their issues... much like my misophonia Facebook page. I'm empathetic, and I let them know I'm struggling with what they're struggling with.

Be sure to point to your website regularly.

Make sure your website is offering something that is valuable enough to warrant filling out a form so you can get basic contact information. This will allow you to convert your social media followers into audience members that you can help even more. Many will seek help on social media before ever visiting your website. And many will pursue help on a website before ever coming to a service. The process is slow, but keep working your community through the process!

Be careful about email campaigns.

Many people use email marketing improperly, overly informing and promoting. Like social media and websites, good email communication delivers help… never unwanted spam. Ensure your church is CANSPAM compliant so anyone who doesn't want the communication you're offering can leave your list easily. It's the law. Google "CANSPAM" to discover other requirements for your campaigns.

Email is the cheapest communication tool to reach your list, but respect the privilege because someone can leave your list anytime you overdo it.

I get hundreds of emails every day as I'm sure you do, too. I have mail client rules that funnel many of them directly into folders that are deleted automatically. More than 180 billion emails are sent daily, and our inboxes have become a mixture of unwanted and wanted emails. Most people have a love-hate relationship with their email, so don't abuse email. Low open rates (mid-20% for religious emails) show that many emails are simply ignored.

Instead, have a meaningful strategy for deepening your relationship with an audience. Help them; don't annoy them. Consider what your audience is looking for from you, and deliver it as easily and painlessly as possible. Get them to look forward to your email.

Email Tricks

Use great subject lines.

Great subject lines will get people to open your emails. Be sure they speak to either your audience's pain/need or the solution they seek (your thread strategy). Also, include these words for an added boost: new, finally, tips, and tricks. Include numbers (e.g. 3 Top Things). Pretty much, use the same suggestions for writing good blogpost titles.

Make sure your content is short.

No one likes long emails, just like no one enjoys long webpages. Keep them around 50-75 words, and use bullet points. Like any great letter writer knows, the P.S. (postscript) will be more apt to be read than any other part of the email. Why? Because it often reiterates the intent of the entire letter.

Know the purpose of your email!

Know the one thing you want the recipient to do after reading your email. If you aren't clear, don't bother sending the email. It's like talking to someone, and as you walk away, you think, "I wonder what they wanted?" It's worse with email. People perceive that it costs time to read an email, so they want... no, demand... a reward at the end. So make sure you deliver it. Just know what "it" is.

The digital world is changing fast, but great communication isn't. Honor and respect someone for spending time with you, and reward them for taking the time.

It's like a great friendship. But we know that there are few deep friendships because it requires spending time selflessly.

Digital communications is most successful when you think of others first. Honor them.

Be known for great communications.

Discussion #19

What other tools should we be using for our communications?

Are our primary and secondary personas actively using these tools? What preferences do they have for receiving information? Have we asked them?

Does our social media communicate our thread effectively?

Do our email campaigns get opened? The average open rate for a church email is mid-20%; do we beat that? Do we have the ability to know?

Are we CANSPAM compliant?

Want additional information, downloads, and worksheets? Join us at www.beknownbook.com.

20

PUT ON YOUR THREAD GLASSES

In my decades of working in communications, I have found that most people have great ideas that they never put into practice. I'm humbled that you read this book. My prayer is that you'll discover your thread *and* put it into practice.

There's an audience that needs you.

So, do it. Start with your audience, research everything you can about them, and provide a world-class, consistent solution. And you'll find success and a following on your platform!

Then, the goal of a church is to connect the thread to the Scarlet Thread of the gospel.

Putting It into Practice

In Chapter 15, we talked about putting on thread glasses. That concept will truly activate your brand as if you're putting on a pair of imaginary stylish glasses and filtering everything in light of your brand. You fully understand the thread and your audience, so you start looking everywhere for it. You walk through your day, and everything seems different.

Here are five ways your thread glasses will start to change you.

1: You'll concentrate on things that matter.

The terminology "rose-colored glasses" describes people wearing imagery glasses so they see everything positively and ignore the negative stuff. In a similar way, thread glasses will allow you to see everything the way your personas see them while ignoring everything else. You will start understanding what the important things are that you can control or communicate differently. You will stop worrying about all the other things that you can't change or that don't matter. Why? Because your audience is willing to overlook the negative aspects of your church (e.g. old facilities, sub-par preaching, a lack of programs, etc.) to enjoy the positive benefits of your thread. You just have to concentrate on communicating the thread.

2: It'll help you to understand how to advocate better.

Like role playing, you will start to view things through your personas' eyes rather than through yours. Your thread glasses will allow you to start advocating for each group you represent.

Walking through the church on a Sunday morning with your thread glasses on will allow you to experience everything like a first-time visitor or a regular attender (e.g. smells, sights, sounds, etc.).

This will make you extra valuable to your church leadership. If you understand your community so that you can empathize with their concerns, problems, feelings, and goals... *and* you can understand their perceptions of your church... this ability will enable you to listen differently in meetings and guide your leadership, co-workers, and volunteers to understand your personas.

3: The consistency will feel refreshing.

Your thread glasses will let you start seeing things similar to your main benefit and allow you to alter them slightly to align them more closely with your branding language.

Similar to when you purchase a new brand of car, it will feel fresh and different. You, alone, will have this amazing car! Then, as you drive down the street with your new-car glasses on, you realize they're everywhere! How did you miss them before? It's the simple practice of viewing everything differently based on a predetermined filter.

Now that you've finally committed to your thread, you'll put on the thread glasses and realize how many parts of your ministry and language will reinforce your thread. Fan the flame of similarity, and allow those things to bolster your brand and existence in the community. It's more obvious than you'd think!

4: You'll look great.

Sure, the glasses you're choosing to put on are trendy, cool, professional, and awesome from your perspective! But remember how you decided on your thread. The glasses that represent your brand are exactly what your personas are pursuing. This will make you and your ministries incredibly attractive. You'll feel like a comfortable home and a place that cares, loves, and helps them.

Why should you proudly wear your thread glasses? Because they'll allow you to draw your community to your thread and will provide opportunities to share the gospel with those people, many of whom wouldn't normally be attracted to a church.

5: You'll be known for something that matters.

This is the summary. Your thread glasses represent everything that matters to your personas. They lock down your consistent branding visual and beneficial thread message, allowing you to concentrate on the things that matter and to develop a process and strategy to support and encourage them.

Final Words

They'll know we are Christians by our love, so use what you're known for with love. You have the privilege of controlling the communications of your church so that more will be attracted to its message. Love your congregation, and love your community.

Then, point your thread to the benefits of having faith in the One who supplies life more abundant than we could ever ask or think.

Go and make disciples with the power that exists within you. Be known for something.

Discussion #20

Do we all wear thread glasses as we go about our church lives?

Are we constantly trying to tie our communications to our thread? How can we do better?

Are we trying to keep it fresh and different so our community and congregation will be attracted to it? How can we make sure?

Are we regularly advocating for our audiences? How can we do better?

How can we make sure our thread continues to connect to Jesus, the gospel, and love?

Want additional information, downloads, and worksheets? Join us at www.beknownbook.com.

ENDNOTES

[1] U.S. Patent and Trademark Office, U.S. Patent Statistic Church (Calendar Years 1963 - 2015),
http://www.uspto.gov/web/offices/ac/ido/oeip/taf/us_stat.htm.

[2] Mary Bellis, "The History of Soaps and Detergents," *About Money*, (Updated Aug 14, 2016), http://inventors.about.com/library/inventors/blsoap.htm.

[3] Information of Human Emotions, "List of Human Emotions" (2017), http://www.listofhumanemotions.com.

[4] Alexandra Sifferlin, "Mental Health: Human Emotions Are Not as Complex as We Thought," *Time*, February 05, 2014, http://time.com/4649/human-emotions-not-as-complex-as-we-think/.

[5] Louise Story, *The New York Times*, "Anywhere the Eye Can See, It's Likely to See an Ad," January 15, 2007, http://www.nytimes.com/2007/01/15/business/media/15everywhere.html?pagewanted=all&_r=0.

CPSIA information can be obtained
at www.ICGtesting.com
Printed in the USA
FFOW05n1125010417

9 781940 024981